Is Calvinism and the TULIP Biblical?

James Battell

Published by James Battell, 2024.

IS CALVINISM AND THE TULIP BIBLICAL?

First edition. January 31, 2024.

ISBN: 979-8224298143

Written by James Battell.

Also by James Battell

The Shocking History of the Jesuits (The Society of Jesus)

King James I of England: The King The Vatican Could Not Kill

The Hidden Truth About Freemasonry, The Catholic Church, And The Illuminati

Bible Prophecy Made Simple For Serious Students of Scripture

Did The Catholic Church Order Abraham Lincoln's Assassination?

Is Calvinism and the TULIP Biblical?

The Book of Genesis Commentary (Chapters 1-11)

Watchman Nee, Witness Lee, and Living Stream Ministry: A Critical Analysis of Their Identity as Cult or Church

What Is Speaking In Tongues And Is It Still For Today?

Ephesians KJV Bible Commentary

The Book of Romans Commentary

Philemon Bible Study (Slavery In Scripture)

The Holy Ghost Within The Trinity

The Immaculate Conception ("Deception")

The Book of John KJV Commentary

The Book of Matthew KJV Commentary

The Epistles of John (1-3 John KJV Commentary)

Agent of Grace

Oliver Cromwell: The Last King of England
The Incredible Story of How the Papacy Became Infallible
Under Pius IX and XII
The Book of Luke KJV Commentary
Billy Graham: The Vatican's Right Hand Man

Table of Contents

Introduction

That God is almighty and all-powerful is not questionable. That man is held responsible for his life and sin is also not questionable. Both views are clearly presented in Holy Scripture; hence we are automatically left with something that seems totally irreconcilable to the finite human mind: how can God be God if man is man? Or in other words, how can God be sovereign if man has a free will?

If man has a free will, is God still God? If God is omnipotent, then man is subject to God, not vice versa, or as the late Calvinist R.C. Sproul puts it: "My children have free wills. When our wills clash I have the authority to overrule their wills. Their wills are to be subordinate to my will; my will is not subordinate to theirs" (Sproul, p. 43).

Sproul's analogy is flawed in at least two ways. Firstly, as a mortal man with finite knowledge, he doesn't have complete access or knowledge of all the pros or cons of any given situation before he decides what to do. For example, had he booked an all-inclusive non-refundable holiday for his family to the Caribbean, hoping and expecting with no proof that on the day he and his family would even be healthy and fit to travel, only to discover on the day of their departure one of his children had a very high fever, not to mention a contagious cough too, he would be forced to postpone if not cancel the family vacation all together. His will over his children in this situation is totally irrelevant. He would be forced to rethink his family's plans.

Secondly, should one of his children when they grow up decide to marry somebody of another faith or no faith, refuse to attend school or college, take up painting and not preaching, his will in this situation would also be totally irrelevant. As a normal man, he would be very limited in almost every situation in life. Yes, he could in certain situations get his own way but this would be very restricted and time-limited, and would also depend on his wife's view and thinking at that given time. And because his comprehension of foreknowledge is also very limited, unlike the Lord's, his argument and analogy, therefore, fails to make any logical sense.

More on the subject of foreknowledge later.

The following verses clearly present this Biblical paradox of man's accountability and God's supremacy, which is based on His foreknowledge: "The Son of man goeth as it is written of him [written in time and according to God's foreknowledge]: but woe unto that man by whom the Son of man is betrayed! it had been good for that man if he had not been born" [man's personal accountability] (Matthew 26:24).

"Him, being delivered by the determinate counsel and foreknowledge of God [God's foreknowledge], ye have taken, and by wicked hands have crucified and slain" [man's personal accountability] (Acts 2:23).

While the Bible presents this paradoxical view of God and man working together to further God's plan of redemption – whether man is aware of this or not (Genesis 50:20; John 11:50-52) – what the Bible doesn't support is the strange 16th century ideology which is called "Calvinism."

To help us understand this further, may I share the following and very helpful explanation, from William Lane Craig: "From God's foreknowledge of a free action, one may infer only that that action will occur, not that it must occur. The agent performing the action has the power to refrain, and were the agent to do so, God's foreknowledge would have been different. Agents cannot bring it about both that God foreknows their action and that they do not perform the action, but this is no limitation on their freedom. They are free either to act or to refrain, and whichever they choose, God will have foreknown. For God's knowledge, though chronologically prior to the action, is logically posterior to the action and determined by it. Therefore, divine foreknowledge and human freedom are not mutually exclusive (Craig, *The Only Wise God*, p. 74).

Even Sproul is honest enough to accept that the Reformers could all be wrong with their Reformed system which includes their eschatological and soteriology beliefs: "To be sure, it is possible that Augustine, Aquinas, Luther, Calvin, and Edwards could all be wrong on this matter" (Sproul, p. 15).

Bizarrely, Sproul seems to think the mystic Thomas Aquinas was a Christian! (He was, in fact, a Roman Catholic, and one that has also been canonised by his church, meaning Catholics can pray to him and other departed "saints" for "intercessions" and so on.)

Not only were these men all wrong, as this book will prove,

but Martin Lloyd-Jones, the famous Welsh preacher of the 20th century, who (I was personally informed by the late Dr Theodore C. Danson) changed his Reformed view on eschatology and embraced the dispensational teaching on the pre-tribulation Rapture, seven-year Tribulation, and the glorious Millennial Reign of the Lord Jesus Christ on the earth. In fact, Theodore told me how Lloyd-Jones had sadly neglected the subject of eschatology until very late in his life, and once he correctly understood it, he happily embraced it.

When I began researching Calvin and his legacy, back in 2004, I tried to be as impartial and as open-minded to this French philosopher as possible. I read many books both for and against Calvin and, therefore, my hope is that this book will be as faithful to the man, his legacy, and theology as is possible.

Calvin's disciples

John Piper: "The Doctrines of Grace [TULIP] are the warp and woof of the Biblical Gospel cherished by so many saints for centuries."

Charles Spurgeon: "I do not ask whether you believe in Calvinism, it is possible you may not, but I believe you will before you enter heaven; I am persuaded as God may have washed your heart, He will wash your brains before you enter heaven."

Such comments as these are breathtaking! Yet wasn't it Spurgeon, saved over thirty years, who wrote the following, when commenting on Psalm 87: "May it be our happy lot to be numbered with the Lord's chosen... let us pray, then, for the adoption and regeneration which will secure us a place among the heaven born"?

Now, isn't this amazing!? Spurgeon was no doubt one of England's most famous and popular preachers of his generation, and yet he didn't know whether or not he was saved. What an absolute and avoidable tragedy!

According to David Samuel, "Arminianism, it has been said, is the back door to Romanism" (Samuel, *The Church in Crisis*, p. 132).

So, if one is not a five-point Calvinist, then they are at best a sympathiser to Roman Catholicism or at worst an agent, consciously or unconsciously, for the Jesuits? More nonsense, of course!

The writer of *True Wisdom Has Two Sides – Calvinism – is it Biblical?* believes Calvinism is another gospel, which would mean it is a false gospel; therefore, a curse from God is on them and their proponents (Billton, p. 114).

The following quote from Calvinist John Bratt is simply breathtaking: "[Calvin was] the stone which the builders had rejected" (Bratt, *The Life and Teachings of John Calvin*, p. 32). Such an appalling comparison to the Lord Jesus Christ should make today's Calvinists cringe with horror, when they see their fellow brethren in times past trying to draw comparisons between Calvin's initial rejection by the people of Geneva and the Jews' rejection of their Messiah!

However, not all people agree with this statement recorded by Philip Schaff: "Gross hypocrite, thou and thy companions will gain little by your pains. If you do not save yourselves by flight, nobody shall prevent your overthrow, and you will curse the hour when you left your monkery" (Schaff, *History of the Christian Church*, Vol. 8, p. 502).

A Masonic infiltration?

"Freemasonry, far from declining, has been spreading. Most alarming, perhaps, is its penetration deep and wide into the established reformed churches and the new ground it is breaking into the Evangelical fellowships of this and other lands" (McCormick, *Christ, The Christian & Freemasonry*, p. 16).

Not only have the Freemasons infiltrated some Reformed churches but according to Adam Weishaupt, the former Jesuit-trained turned Illuminati supremo: "The most wonderful thing of all is that the distinguished Lutheran and Calvinist theologians who belong to our order really believe that they see in it [Illuminati] the true and genuine sense of Christian religion. Oh, mortal man, is there anything you cannot be made to believe?"

As I cannot verify if the above quote is authentic, may I suggest to those in Reformed churches, or any church for that matter, to ask their pastors whether or not any of them are Freemasons or members of the Illuminati? And if they are not, what is their view on Christians who are members? And more importantly, what is their position on Freemasonry in general? You may be surprised not only by what they say, but what they don't say! And while you're in the "pastor's office," ask him/her what they think about the Catholic Church and the ecumenical movement. Again, you may be surprised by their reply.

Who was the real John Calvin?

When Calvin was only three years old or so, his mother died, leaving his father with the sole responsibility of raising young John and his other siblings. Once his father remarried, two new daughters from his second marriage were added to the Calvin clan.

His parents were wealthy, well thought of and dedicated Catholics. Their children enjoyed a comfortable and privileged upbringing.

Calvin was a bright young man and highly thought of in his Catholic and even royal environment.

Calvin the student

As a dazzling student in Paris, Calvin encountered the following grim conditions welcoming French students, as described by Reyburn: "They contained no accommodation for the students, so the students had to find their own lodgings. These, for the most part, were execrable. A slum in a modern city is clean and sweet compared with the filthy lanes they were situated in. As there was no supervision, life for them was free and easy, not to say disreputable, and the students were often in bad odour with the citizens... rising before five in the morning... picked their way through mud and puddles to the room where the professor awaited them... went to their lodgings...or to the wine shop to find relief from their drudgery... Erasmus says that in the college he attended, in a year's time, by wretched lodgings, bad and spare diet, late and hard studies, of many young men of genius, some were killed, some went mad, some became infected with loathsome diseases, and all were brought into danger" (Reyburn, H.Y. *John Calvin, His Life, Letters and Work*, p. 9).

Calvin the diplomat

De Greef writes extensively about Calvin's relationship with the royals: "He stayed for a few weeks in Ferrara among kindred spirits at the court of the reform-minded Duchess Renata (Renee of France), daughter of King Louis XII of France and sister-in-law of King Francis I" (De Greef, *The Writings of John Calvin*, p. 26).

"On July 25, 1541, Marguerite of Angouleme, Queen of Navarre, wrote Calvin a letter of thanks in the name of her brother Francis I because during the religious colloquy in Worms he, together with Melanchthon and Bucer, had urged Philip of Hesse (alas, in vain) to forge an alliance between the German princes and the king of France against Charles V. Such an alliance would have brought an end to the persecution of the French Protestants" (De Greef, p. 40).

Of all the Reformers, Calvin was the most prolific writer. Each of his Biblical commentaries would be dedicated to dukes, queens and even kings. His commentaries on James, Peter I, II, and Jude were presented to King Edward VI of England. His commentary on Isaiah would also be offered to the king personally, by one Nicolas de la Fontaine (De Greef, p. 99).

"It is a grand thing to be king, especially of such a country, but I have no doubt that you place an incomparably greater value on being a Christian. Thus God has conferred upon you the still greater, inestimable privilege of being a Christian king, indeed of being allowed to serve him as 'lieutenant' in the maintenance of the kingdom of Jesus Christ in England... the good understanding between Edward VI and Calvin can be seen from the fact that the king paid Calvin a hundred crowns as thanks for the writings he had received" (De Greef, p. 111).

Calvin blamed John Knox for Queen Elizabeth's rejection of Calvin's revised commentary on Isaiah, for Knox had previously written against female rulership, for which the queen was naturally opposed to such a position.

The queen thought that Calvin shared Knox's view (which he didn't) and, therefore, relations between London and Geneva were strained even more (De Greef, p. 104).

Calvin and his family

De Greef goes on to describe that Calvin's second marriage lasted only nine years, as his wife and their son (who was only a few days old) both died in March 1549. Calvin would go on to adopt her other two children from her first marriage.

Was history sadly repeating itself again?

Two members of Calvin's family were excommunicated from the Catholic Church; one being his uncle, a Catholic priest, and the other his father, due to views deemed "heretical" by Rome. Catholics were so worried in those days about burying excommunicated relatives that Calvin's brother Charles had the delicate task of negotiating with the cathedral to allow a Catholic burial for their late father (De Greef, p. 22).

Before Calvin's father died, he instructed John to abandon his studies in philosophy and begin legal studies instead (Reyburn, p. 12). Naturally, Calvin listened to his father's counsel, but in his heart he wanted to be a philosopher, so after his father's death, and upon finishing his legal studies, he returned to his philosophical work (Reyburn, p. 15).

Calvin had once been a humanist, and like Luther, law was something both men had trained for, prior to going into full-time ministry (Mumford, *The Condition of Man*, p. 188).

Is Calvin's conversion credible?

Only once in his commentary on the Psalms does Calvin mention his conversion. Oddly, he would go on to say how he didn't know for sure when he was saved/converted from Catholicism (Irwin, *John Calvin, The Man and His Work*, pp. 108-109).

Professor Lefranc, in his book *La Jeunesse de Calvin*, thinks that: "Though the decision may have been sudden at the end, the conversion was a gradual process." However, one of his contemporaries, Pieter Bloccius, wondered if Calvin was ever saved: "They who recommend that heretics be put to death show that they are not truly regenerate... this you have not learned from Christ, who rebuked the vengeful disciples." (Billton, pp. 51-52).

Throughout this book, you will see how most of Calvin's critics are ironically from the Reformed/Calvinist camp.

Billton adds, "So, it would appear that the man whom many today take as their spiritual guide was regarded, and understandably so, by some of his contemporaries, as not being born again" (Billton, p. 52).

Calvin and Augustine's unfortunate 'partnership'

According to Bilton, Calvin leaned very much on his hero Augustine for much of his theology (even though Augustine knew no Hebrew or Greek; p. 43), for both men (even though they lived over a thousand years apart) wanted to set up their own man-made kingdom of God on earth, but without King Jesus on the throne. The only difference was that Augustine's kingdom would have been "a Catholic city of God," whereas Calvin's would have been "a Calvinists' city of God."

Billton also offers the following on this rehash of Augustinism: "Calvin resurrected Augustine's teaching, which was rejected by the early church as unacceptable and heretical" (p. 9).

"From the Greek Fathers he received the doctrines of the Trinity and the Person of Christ. From the Latin Fathers and especially from Augustine, he took his doctrines of Man, of Sin, and of Grace. From Luther he derived the doctrine of Justification by Faith" (Reyburn, p. 350).

"John Calvin was part of a long line of thinkers who based their doctrine of predestination on the Augustinian interpretation of St. Paul" (Muller, *Christ and the Decree*, p. 22).

"There is hardly a doctrine of Calvin that does not bear the marks of Augustine's influence" (Baker, *Berkouwer's Doctrine of Election: Balance or Imbalance?*)

In Calvin's *Institutes of the Christian Religion*, which he wrote in the south of France in 1534, he quotes Augustine over 400 times, and goes on to call him "holy father," and proudly says of him: "Augustine is so wholly with me, that if I wished to write a confession of my faith, I could do so with all fullness and satisfaction to myself out of his writings" (Vance, p. 104).

Calvin was so besotted with Augustine that he dubbed himself, "an Augustinian theologian" (see introduction to Calvin's *Institutes*, p. 1303, IX, xiv. 26). Even Luther was addressed as "my revered father" (De Greef, p. 138).

Yet, I cannot help but note that such admiration would not have been recompensed back to Calvin from Augustine!

It must also be mentioned that Calvin's initial purpose was to reform the Church of Rome, not to reject it. The same was true of Martin Luther. "They [the Reformers] never doubted the validity of the Catholic ordinances, and rejected the idea of re-baptism" (Schaff, Vol. 8, p. 313).

Some might be forgiven for wondering if Calvin simply plagiarised much of Augustine's popular work and successfully passed it off as his own.

Augustine and his anti-Biblical theology

After the apostle Peter and Thomas Aquinas, Aurelius Augustine is probably Catholicism's greatest "saint" in their church. He was the son of a pagan father, but his mother, "St." Monica was a Christian (probably safer to say Catholic). This African Catholic from Algeria was seen very much as the founder and architect of today's Roman Catholic Church.

His road to Catholicism is an interesting one. After converting to Manichaeism (a period which lasted 8 years), he then lost interest in this pagan religion, so left for Rome. He was very much taken in by pagan philosophers, upon arrival. It's stated that during a period of great testing, Augustine claimed to hear a child's voice, under a fig tree, which allegedly told him to "Take up and read."

Augustine would go on to make many theological errors and blunders, which regrettably to this day, have remained in Christendom.

In S. Baring Gould's book *The Evangelical Revival,* he says the following: "With his new dogmas Augustine introduced a whole category of new terms, "Universal human depravity," "Original sin," "Effectual calling," and God's irreversible "Decrees." Novel altogether Augustine's doctrine was. He was the first in Christ's Church to deny that Christ died for all men, to deny to man the exercise of free will, to urge on the persecution of heretics to death, to exalt slavery as a divine institution, to forge a theology so cruel, so shocking, that he himself, as he contemplated his accomplished work, stood aghast at its hideous completeness. He was actually, truly an innovator altering the whole character of Christianity" (Billton, p. 44).

Augustine taught infant sprinkling was essential for salvation (Augustine, *On the Merits and Forgiveness of Sins* 1.23-26-34), and he believed that unbaptized infants who died at birth would go to Hell if they hadn't been baptized in time (1.35).

Casper Schwenkfeld, however, believed infant baptism was heresy (Schaff, Vol. 7, p. 574, 654, 656), and so did some of the early church "fathers." From 90 to 300 AD, Church historians universally agreed that the doctrine of baptizing infants was not practiced anywhere. For example, Alexandra (254), Hilary of Poitiers (360), Basil of Caesarea (379), Chrysostom (400), Gregory of Nazianzen (386), and Ambrose of Milan (390) all held to adult-only baptisms.

Historians such as G. H. Orchard credit this doctrine and practice to the Roman Catholic Augustine himself.

Ruckman offers us the following on this: "Augustine and Calvin taught that a man got saved by being elected when he was sprinkled, unless he wasn't elect to start with, and then the sprinkling was actually a waste of time."

Roger du Barry, a five-point Calvinist, confirms how the Reformers taught that baptism for infants was essential for their salvation: "This was the position of the entire Reformation (infant baptism for salvation), whether Lutheran or Reformed, Presbyterian or Anglican. They were completely unanimous on this point, and fought vigorously against those who tried to downplay it or turn it in a more baptistic direction. Today, most evangelicals would insist that one enters into the kingdom of God simply by believing the gospel, or making a decision for Christ, without at any time mentioning baptism" (*The Journal of the Church of England Continuing*, December 2004, p. 10).

For more information on infant salvation, please see the "Unconditional election" section below.

Augustine said that nobody could be completely sure of salvation, and only through the Catholic Church, with all its pagan sacraments, could one ever hope to be saved! This would differ from the Protestant Reformers' belief that one is saved by grace alone, through faith alone, in Christ alone. Of course, Augustine never held to the Reformers' doctrine of justification by faith alone, even though many of them totally missed that the Bible teaches baptism for adult believers only. He also called for the death of those teaching this *damnable heresy!* This is something famous Calvinist preachers' today conveniently refuse to share with their theological students and church members.

Again, when examining the major theological differences between Augustine and Calvin, it's almost comical to try and fathom why Calvin repeatedly praised and fought so hard to credit and align himself with Augustine. Yet, had Calvin lived in the days of Augustine, he almost certainly would have been executed, possibly even on the orders of Augustine, no less.

Calvinist William Cunningham said of Augustine's view on salvation: "[It was] defective and erroneous."

Augustine also believed that the Septuagint was divinely inspired. He said the Apocrypha was canonical, even though he acknowledged the Jews rejected it. He wrote to Jerome asking him to translate the Old Testament from the Greek Septuagint and not from Hebrew.

Augustine once held the view that man had freewill, and he also advocated violence and death towards "heretics," i.e., Bible-believing Christians and all non-Catholics (Schaff, Vol. 3, p. 144).

One group that was persecuted the most were the Donatists. One of his victims said the following of Augustine: "The Lord Jesus Christ, the Saviour of souls, sent fishermen, not soldiers, for the propagation of his gospel."

Billton also adds to this: "Calvin seems to have forgotten that the Lord Jesus Christ was put to death by religious people who believed Christ to be a blasphemer, because He claimed to be the Son of God" (Billton, p. 49).

Augustine also:

Followed Ambrose and allegorised large portions of Scripture.

Stated that Satan had been bound in Hell since the Church was formed, and would only be loosed at the end of the world.

Believed that the Church was the Kingdom of God, and that it is now reigning.

Stated that Isaiah 35 was fulfilled in the Catholic Church.

Falsely date-fixed Jesus' return to 1000 AD (*City of God*, Book XX, Chapters 7, 9, 13).

Said Israel would never return to their land.

Taught the authority of tradition and the Catholic Church being the sole authority of interpreting the Bible.

Said Mary was sinless and advocated worship of her (Schaff, Vol. 3, p. 1021).

Believed in the intercession of the saints and adoration of relics.

Is credited for establishing the pernicious and lucrative doctrine of purgatory (Boettner, *Immortality*, p. 135).

Took the odd view that all sex was sinful if not used for procreation.

Followed the Mormon line that polygamy over monogamy was acceptable, if used for propagation (Augustine, *On Christian Doctrine*, 3.18.27).

Alarming facts on Calvin

Calvin correctly said that the Lord has not given any one person full insight into everything (De Greef, p. 95). While he should be credited for eliciting certain truths for the Body of Christ during and after the Reformation, it must be said, however, that he remained rather shortsighted; for he seemed to look only as far back as Augustine for much of his theology, and not the word of God.

May I quote a Puritan pastor, John Robinson whose views are, I believe, very relevant for then and today: "I bewail the condition of the Reformed churches...the Lutherans cannot be drawn to go beyond what Luther saw. And the Calvinists, as you see, stick where Calvin left them...Luther and Calvin were precious shining lights. Yet God did not reveal His whole to them...I am very confident that the Lord hath more truth and light yet to break forth out of His Holy Word" (Drummond, *The Story of American Protestantism*, p. 51).

Much of what this Puritan pastor said is correct. But tradition, whether Catholic or Protestant, has the unfortunate habit of hindering one's salvation, and also stunting one's growth in Christ.

Calvin also:

Was offered the role as chief pastor of St. Peter's Cathedral in Geneva, with 250 gallons of wine a year thrown in.

Considered the attacks on his character and doctrine to be

equivalent to what the apostle Paul suffered (Calvin, *A Defence of the Secret Providence of God*, p. 292).

Bizarrely compared himself to Ezekiel, when he offered the following: "Because they did not know that a prophet was in their midst" (De Greef, p. 150).

Never afforded himself a holiday and took little interest in money (Irwin, p. 118).

"While studying at the College of Montaigu, he would regularly study till midnight, eat a little dinner, awake early the next morning, revise what he had studied the night before, and then begin his next day... his carelessness about bodily exercise and regular food made serious inroads on his vitality, and created the dyspepsia and nervous irritability that tormented him increasingly all the rest of his life" (Reyburn, p. 13).

This same author says Calvin had a retentive memory, from all the years of hard and dedicated study.

Calvin wasn't paid by the church but by the state. Upon his return to Geneva, he was offered one house with a nice garden, and a generous stipend of 500 florins per annum.

He had little interest in eschatology: "Calvin is the least satisfactory of all the Protestant leaders regarding prophecies in general" (Schaff, Vol. 7, p. 295). In fact, he failed to understand the book of Revelation (McNeill, *The History and Character of Calvinism*, p. 153) and called the idea of a thousand-year reign of Christ "childish" (Calvin, *Institutes*, p. 995, III.xxx.5).

Luther, on the other hand, desperately hoped Christ's return would be less than a hundred years away (Kerr, *A Compend of Luther's Theology*, p. 245). Yet Luther also ridiculed the Millennial Reign as "a dream."

Calvin was ecumenical and said the following about Protestant unity: "And so, according to the rule of Scripture, to bring the separated Churches into one, neither labour nor trouble of any kind or to be spared" (Irwin, p. 147).

He also made a peculiar statement concerning God's effectual calling: "Yet sometimes He also causes those whom He illuminates for a time to partake of it; then he justly forsakes them on account of their ingratiate and strikes them with even greater blindness."

Not only is this unscriptural and sounds rather Islamic, but the whole structure of his system contradicts this, for Billton offers an explanation as to how the Calvinist concept of "irresistible grace" works: "Whom He gives grace cannot reject it, and the rest being reprobate cannot accept it" (Billton, p. 54).

Moreover, Calvin:

Believed 2 Peter was divinely inspired, but questioned if Peter had written all of it (Irwin, p. 99).

Retained invocation of purgatory and the saints (Irwin, p. 12).

Never believed there were grounds for Christians to leave church fellowship.

Stated that communion was to be dispensed at every meeting

that was held, or at least once a week.

Believed two "sacraments" helped with salvation: baptism and the Lord's Supper (Irwin, p. 72; Vance, p. 110). Those who opposed this unbiblical view were called "frantic spirits and mad beasts" and were to be severely persecuted.

Roger de Barry, again toeing the Reformed line, adds further thought to Calvin's foaming rhetoric: "For this reason they [the Reformers] considered the denial of baptism to the children of believers to be a great sin, worthy of severe punishment by excommunication, as well as active from civil magistrate. *To deny baptism to a Christian child is to deny it salvation,* just as failure to circumcise a Jewish child resulted in its excommunication from the people" (*The Journal of the Church of England Continuing,* April 2005, p. 16) (italics added).

There are several problems with the above summary, but I will only list two of them.

Circumcision in the Old Testament was only for boys, never girls. Moreover, circumcision was carried out on the boy before he had even come of age, which meant simply that the newborn child was now a member of the commonwealth of Israel, based on the faith on his parents. Also if Mr. Barry shares this view of the Reformers, it isn't lost on us how he conveniently omitted "boy" and substituted the word "child" in his false premise!

As has already been stated, this act was for the nation of Israel only, and was for men, never women. Therefore, it cannot be understood to be essential for salvation, for if it were, then only men would be saved.

Abraham was saved before he was circumcised, not after. And all the men who wandered in the desert for forty years were not circumcised until Joshua 5:2-7.

In the New Testament, faith comes first, followed by baptism. But baptism will not save anyone. Like circumcision, it is symbolic, and as such, should be remembered as such.

I would also add that if circumcision were needed for salvation, then Miriam (Moses' sister) and Mary (the Lord's mother) would both have been lost. This type of poor exegesis is also found in relation to some New Testament verses, as some groups of people have come to a flawed conclusion that unless women have children, they *cannot be saved* (1 Timothy 2:15).

And what of Lydia (Acts 16:14) or Anna (Luke 2:36)? Were they damned too?

I suggest that the Reformers were still stuck and indoctrinated with this erroneous and almost obsession with water baptism somehow "aiding sinners" into Heaven! One can only wonder why they never broke free from it!

Calvin would also oppose the idea of "laypeople" baptizing infants and would oppose the idea of women baptizing children. Augustine again is cited for this (De Greef, p. 216).

His opposition to laypeople baptizing infants, and possibly adults as well, was no doubt down to his stubborn refusal to recognise laypeople in principle having any direct role in the local assembly, much like his Catholic counterparts, for he would not want to relinquish power over the people at all.

Regarding the Lord's Supper, Calvin believed that not only was Christ's body spiritually and really present during communion (Vance, p. 107), but also that the supper was the "sacrament" to help us to live a Christian life (De Greef, p. 134).

This doctrine is rather similar to the mass, for Catholics not only believe they were born again when first baptized/christened as infants, but they are being born again each time they receive their "sacrament."

Calvin also seems to have adopted a confused view. How can the breaking of bread be spiritual and literal?

Like baptism, he seems to have retained more Catholic doctrine.

The three main leaders of the Reformation disagreed with one another on the actual substance of communion.

Luther believed in consubstantiation (a middle view from where Rome stands).

Zwingli correctly understood it to be a commemoration, although Calvin said of this opinion: "[it is] false and pernicious" (Wendel, *Calvin: Origins and Development of His Religious Thought,* p. 333).

Additionally, Calvin:

Reinstated "confirmation" for youths. Bishops would lay hands on those being baptized (Irwin, p. 73).

Was arrested and re-arrested many times for his dogmatic stand on theology, before returning to Geneva.

Wrote his first edition of the *Institutes* in Latin (Irwin, p. 26-27), when he was just 26 years of age (Billton, p. 44).

Praised the pagan writings of Plato and Aristotle (Irwin, p. 34, 44).

Said Adam had a free will (Irwin, p. 36; 44).

Taught that Jesus, upon death, went to Hell: "Bore in His soul the torture of condemned and ruined men" (Irwin, p. 59).

It's not clear if he held this heresy to the same extent as Benny Hinn, Joyce Meyer and most "Word of Faith" preachers, who say that Jesus was then born again in Hell.

When he returned to Geneva, immorality was everywhere (Irwin, p. 81). While exiled from Geneva, due to his financial burdens, he had to sell his books and take in lodgers to get by (Irwin, p. 100).

Calvin was called "the pope of Protestantism" by Church historian and five-point Calvinist Philip Schaff (Herrick, *Some Heretics of Yesterday*, p. 295). He was also very much a philosopher at heart, and was hounded and persecuted by local mobs, not for his soul-winning, but because of his aspirations to be an ecclesiastical dictator.

Calvin and Ignatius Loyola were both in Paris in 1528,

studying at the same college.

While Calvin was writing *Institutes*, Loyola was founding the Jesuits.

When Calvin was organising his theological training academy and college in Geneva, Loyola was establishing similar institutions for training students and provocateurs in Rome. Before Calvin died, he had sent preachers of the reformed faith into every country in Western Europe. Loyola on the other hand had a thousand centers of activity in Italy alone" (Reyburn, p. 12).

Calvin enjoyed playing quoits and a table game called clef, and performed a play, probably of the Passion, in Geneva on 8 April 1546 (Irwin, p. 124).

In Geneva, the Lord's Supper was observed four times a year. In Calvin's own church, it was observed once a month (Irwin, p. 130).

By 1540, the style of church worship was as follows:

Invocation

Confession of sins and absolution

Reading of the Scriptures followed by singing

Free prayer

Sermon

Long prayer followed by the Lord's Prayer

Congregational signing followed by a benediction.

Moreover, the church upheld the office and titles of paid bishops and archbishops (Irwin, p. 131).

Calvin's new "City of God"

On 1 May 1541, the Council of Geneva revoked their ban on the exclusion of Calvin from Geneva, and subsequently wrote to him seeking his return.

Even so, after a period of absence, Calvin wasn't too keen to return, and wouldn't rush to respond to this formal request either. However, he did grudgingly return on 25 August 1541.

Problems soon arose, for Calvin found himself at odds on many occasions when it came to who had the final say on matters such as excommunication, and those able to partake in the Lord's Supper. Calvin won some battles, whilst the Council won others.

On the subject of excommunication, Calvin wrote victoriously to Heinrich Bullinger: "Recently, it was finally decided after a long struggle that the right to excommunication belongs to us" (De Greef, p. 45).

By 1559, Calvin's academy had trained 2,000 men to go back to France and teach against Roman Catholicism. The academy was nicknamed "the seminary of death." Many of them were murdered by the Catholics. His educational system was free but mandatory. It was later imitated by the Jesuits, who were also copied by the Nazis during the Second World War (Irwin, p. 141).

Calvin was also credited for initiating justice in courts for victims and assailants, and a decent system of education. By the time of his death, 1,200 scholars had been registered with his university, with 300 students, two of them being John Knox and James Arminius (Irwin, p. 140).

Calvin conducted his way of religion, much like that of a church-state, and believed that his "city of God" was a theocracy (Irwin, p. 136).

Elders from the churches also enjoyed a seat in the civil courts (Irwin, p. 135), a bit like the Anglican bishops enjoy in the House of Lords in England.

Around 13,000 people lived in Geneva, with 5,000 being foreigners. If one wished to live there, they would have to take an oath of loyalty, and then live according to the Reformation and be obedient and subject to them (Irwin, p. 139). For those who agreed with the Reformer, life must have been good. However, for those who disagreed with him, living under such tyranny couldn't have been easy (Vance, p. 87).

Church attendance was mandatory. All were to publicly denounce blasphemers and dishonest persons in their midst (Irwin, p. 139). If one converted to Catholicism, he would forfeit his citizenship (Irwin, p. 139). Calvin inherited much of this framework, which dated back to the Dark Ages but chose, along with the town officials, not only to retain it, but to revive it (Vance, p. 88).

Schaff offers his thoughts on this "churchocracy": "It was a glaring inconsistency that those who had just shaken off the yoke of popery as an intolerable burden, should subject their conscience and intellect to a human creed; in other words, substitute for the old Roman popery a modern Protestant popery" (Schaff, Vol. 8, p. 357).

Another Calvinist writer acknowledged that Calvin's stringent manmade rules were unacceptable: "Calvin thus denied and violated the rights of conscience and personal liberty in private life and in matters of religion – a deplorable but natural consequence of his contempt for and denial of man's free will in his general doctrine" (Guizort, *Great Christians of France*, p. 267).

Calvin persecuted anybody who questioned his authority and philosophy

"Power corrupts, and absolute power corrupts absolutely."

Tragically, this was true in the case of Calvin's police state. And Ruckman echoes this sentiment: "Calvin wanted to be a king, issuing orders to people. That is why he was in Geneva, and that is what he did" (Ruckman, p. 33).

When any of the Reformers are mentioned, Calvin's name is forever associated with his brutal method of putting down those who opposed him and his theological views. If he wasn't to blame for the persecution himself, he certainly would have been aware of it; therefore, he is still accountable for his part, whether directly or indirectly, for he could have left Geneva due to its tyrannical method of enforcing Protestantism on its subjects.

Calvinist writer C. H. Irwin states that he condoned torture and death of "heretics" (Irwin, p. 28).

However, his brutal legacy didn't die with him, for alas, his faithful followers would continue in his steps, in their desire to set up Reformed churches throughout Britain and Europe.

In the 17th century, Episcopalians and Presbyterians in England were almost all Calvinistic (Irwin, p. 152). The Church of England, funded and controlled to some extent by Parliament during the 16th century, forced Calvinism on all its subjects. Refusal to accept this resulted in reprimands, imprisonments, and in some cases, death.

The Presbyterians would dominate the Church of England during this period.

All who denied God, the Scripture and the final judgment were to suffer the pains of death.

The Westminster Assembly was also funded and controlled by Parliament, with Presbyterians once again having the final say on all issues. Other Christian groups were strictly prohibited.

Religious freedom, something forever absent in so many Catholic countries during this period, was also absent in the UK during this time. In fact, Calvinists would say the following about those who didn't agree with Calvinism: "the last and strongest hold of Satan."

Non-Calvinists suffered terribly at the hands of Calvinists. Baptists and independents would also be treated with utter contempt, with some being called "mortal enemies of the state church."

"Many thousands of [Anabaptists] were martyred by the Roman Catholic church and they suffered a great deal of persecution at the hands of the reformers, because they did not accept the doctrine of either Luther, Calvin or Zwingli and opposed the link of church and government" (Billton, p. 15).

Calvinist Samuel Rutherford was also swept up during this time of extreme censorship and mind control and would say the following: "There is but one true church and all that are outside of it are heretics who must be destroyed."

"There is but one true church and all that are outside of it are heretics who must be destroyed."

Where have we heard this type of foaming rhetoric before?

"That the present Catholic Roman Church is the Church founded by Christ and attested by Scripture and tradition; that she, and she alone, is the heir to the promises of Christ and the ark of salvation" (Addis, *A Catholic Dictionary*, p. 168).

Most notable deaths under Calvinists' rule:

Jacques Gruet was beheaded on 26 July 1547, with the consent of Calvin (De Greef, p. 47).

Jerome Bolsec, a Genevan doctor who publicly criticised Calvin's views on predestination, was cautioned and threatened with the whip, should he return to Geneva, for he had been forced to leave due to his "erroneous views" on Calvinism. Bolsec would go so far as to draw comparisons between the god of Jupiter and the god of Calvinism: "(They make God) a tyrant, and in fact an idol, as the pagans made of Jupiter" (*Register of Geneva*, pp. 137-138).

Giovanni Valentino Gentilis, who opposed the Trinity, was sentenced to death. This ruling would later be overturned by the council, but he would go on to break the terms of his release from custody, and on 10 September 1558, under the jurisdiction of Bern, was beheaded (De Greef, p. 180).

It has been claimed that 60 people were burnt alive at the stake in Calvin's theocratic city (Hunt, *What Love is This?*)

The cruel torture and killing of Michael Servetus

The most infamous incident, which will be forever associated with Calvin, would have to be the torture and subsequent public execution of the Spaniard Michael Servetus. In fact, I would suggest that when one thinks of Calvin, one cannot help but think of Servetus; much like when one thinks of John F. Kennedy, one thinks of Lee Harvey Oswald.

Interestingly, numerous Calvinists line up to condemn the action of their "reformer-in-chief":

"Calvin burned Servetus" (Farrar, *History of Interpretation*, p. 351).

"When all is understood, admirers of Calvin must still look upon it with shame" (McNeill, p. 347).

"In our judgement Calvin was guilty of sin" (Bratt, p. 41).

So, what exactly were Servetus' crimes? Well, he rejected the Trinity, Christ's eternal Sonship and infant baptism, and he endorsed astrology.

On its own, this is heretical but could never "justifiably" warrant the death penalty.

Servetus was a Spanish linguistic expert who lived in France and studied medicine, and was very much a thorn in the side of Calvin, and the Catholic Church for that matter. The Catholics loathed him for his views on the pope: "O vilest of all beasts, most brazen of harlots," he would say (Vance, p. 91).

Servetus was the first of many people who dubbed Calvin "the pope of Protestantism" and would accuse him of being a sorcerer who should be imprisoned and banished from Geneva (De Greef, p. 176).

Such comments soon landed him in trouble with all branches of Christendom.

His main opponent was Calvin, however, and after extensive correspondence between both parties (Calvin had sent him his *Institutes* to read), Calvin later dissociated himself from him.

Calvin would say of his writings: "[They were] defiled by his vomit" (Schaff, Vol. 8, p. 728).

One thing that has never been explained satisfactorily was why Servetus travelled to Geneva when he must have known death awaited him. Rumours of collusion, however, between Calvin's enemies and Michael Servetus have long existed. According to the Swiss historian Bonnivard, "The enemies of Calvin, who were then governors of the city, by means of the bastard of Geneva, who was the jailer, and was at the same time one of Purrin's partisans, stirred up Servetus against Calvin, giving him the hope of their support, and in this way they persuaded him to not only dispute with Calvin, but to insult him when the magistrates took him into the prison with them" (Reyburn, pp. 179-180). "I am led to believe that these people favour this profane good-for-nothing, because of their hatred to Calvin" (Reyburn, p. 180).

"I am led to believe that these people favour this profane good-for-nothing, because of their hatred to Calvin" (3 p. 180).

Whether this is true or not, one thing is certain: Servetus had crossed the line. His heretical allegations against the word of God, and his prolonged antagonism toward Calvin meant his life now hung in the balance. Geneva, being a self-proclaimed Old Testament-styled theocracy, had the power to enforce the full weight of the Mosaic Law.

Calvin would later write of this period: "I shall never permit him to depart alive, provided my authority be of any avail" (Calvin, *Letters of John Calvin*, p. 174). Calvin: "I hope that sentence of death will at least be passed upon him" (Calvin, *Letters*, p. 82).

So, it was, that Servetus now found himself under arrest. A trial soon followed, which lasted over two months, with Calvin leading the prosecution. He was subsequently found guilty on 27 October 1553, with the charge being publicly read out: "Having a summary of the process against the prisoner, Michael Servetus, and the reports of the parties consulted before us, it is hereby resolved, and in consideration of his great errors and blasphemies decreed, that he shall be taken to Champel, and there burned alive; that his sentence should be carried into effect to-morrow, and that his books (only three have survived today, one being in Edinburgh University, which Calvin once owned) be burned with him" (Reyburn , p. 184).

Calvin first tried to have the mode of death changed to

beheading (De Greef, p. 176), but when this failed, he called for the sword instead (Reyburn, p. 184).

Such "little mercies" from the "reformer-in-chief" have long caused his disciples shame and pain. All these attempts failed, however!

"The council of Geneva therefore turned a deaf ear to Calvin's arguments and ordered its sentence to be carried out" (Reyburn, p. 184).

It should be pointed out that Calvin did try to save the Spaniard before he died, but to no avail (Reyburn, p. 185). Whether this helps Calvin's tarnished reputation or not will need to be decided not only by church historians, but more importantly at the Judgment Seat of Christ (for saved people) or the Great White Throne (for lost people).

After spending considerable time pleading with Servetus to repent, Calvin said, "Then, seeing that my exhortations affected nothing, I did not wish to be wiser than my Master, and, following the commandment of St. Paul, I withdrew from a heretic who was self-condemned" (Reyburn, p. 185).

Again, some in Calvin's own camp are quick to condemn their "reformer-in-chief": "Calvin does not appear well in this. His own words are convincing proof of a coldness and hardness of nature, which, in the sad circumstances, makes him peculiarly unlovable. A sentence of grave regret that a sense of duty compelled him to pursue Servetus to the death, and an appeal that Servetus would forgive him if this sense of duty had led him astray, would have commended him to Servetus and to men of subsequent generations with more effect than this self-righteous lecture" (Reyburn, p. 185).

"On 1 September eleven members of the Council visited Servetus in his cell and took Calvin with him. A theological discussion ensued, which the Councillors cut short, ordering both Servetus and Calvin to set down on paper their leading positions with proofs in support of them" (Reyburn, p. 179).

Servetus' last words were: "O Jesus, Son of the Eternal God, have pity on me" (Vance, p. 91). Some say Servetus' torturous death lasted thirty long minutes. (Reyburn, p. 186), but Billton records it actually lasted some three hours, because they used green wood (Billton, p. 50).

"Calvin never regretted the part he played in the case of Servetus, any more than the public prosecutor regrets the part he played in securing the punishment of a notorious criminal" (Reyburn, p. 187).

In fact, in his book *Fidelis Exposito errorum mich. Serveti*, he argues that Scripture condoned capital punishment. He even quotes the Lord who said: "Compel those to come in" (Luke 14:23), and then attempts to use two other verses (Acts 5:5; 1 Timothy 1:20).

The only problem with these verses is this: In Acts 5, God Himself intervened and death occurred for Ananias and Sapphira. And 1 Timothy 1:20 simply refers to excommunication. Therefore, Calvin is still not exonerated for his awful treatment of this heretic.

It isn't surprising that Calvin once again looks to Augustine for justification for capital punishment to silence Servetus (De Greef, p. 177).

Billton says the following of Augustine: "Through his doctrine [he] has the blood of millions of devout believers in Christ, as well as Jews and Muslims on his hands"! (Billton, p. 42).

A whole 350 years would elapse until the "Calvin faithful" would officially apologise for their beloved leaders' actions. On 27 October 1903, some European and American Calvinists came together to erect a monument in remembrance of Michael Servetus: "Reverent and grateful sons of Calvin, our great Reformer, but condemning an error which was of his age" (Strong, *Systematic Theology*, p. 778).

Legalism and sadism

We also read of the following bizarre accounts of this type of self-proclaimed theocracy, when taken to the extreme: "The wife of Pierre Ameaux... had been condemned for life because of immoral behaviour... the Little Council could not decide between a mild and severe form of punishment... Ameaux had to kneel at the door of the Council and ask Calvin for his forgiveness... Calvin had wanted to visit Ameaux in prison, but was prohibited by the Council... Ameaux had publicly offended God with the assertion that Calvin had been preaching heresy for seven years without the church's intervention. Now Calvin favoured a more severe punishment, namely, that Ameaux in penitential dress, bareheaded, and with a burning torch in his hand, be led from prison to the town hall. Kneeling there between the two doors, he was to beseech God and the tribunal for mercy. Ameaux was sentenced to this public penance on April 8" (De Greef, pp. 45-46).

"A man was banished from the city for three months because he heard an ass bray and said jestingly, 'He prays a beautiful Psalm'... Three men who had laughed during a sermon were imprisoned for three days... Three children were punished because they remained outside of a church to eat some cakes... A child was whipped publicly for calling his mother a thief... A girl who struck her parents was beheaded to vindicate the dignity of the Fifth Commandment... A person was imprisoned for four days because he wanted to call his child Claude [the name of a Catholic saint] instead of Abraham"

(Merle, *The History of the Protestant Church in Hungary*, Vol. VII).

"Those who dissented from them [the Reformers] were not to be tolerated. This included not only Catholics, but that noble group of 'heretics' who thought the Reformers did not go far enough [in their Reformation of the church.] In Zwingli's Zurich they were ordered to have their infants baptized. Rebaptism was made a crime punishable by death. On January 5, 1527, Felix Manz was bound and thrown in the river by the Zurich authorities because he had become involved in Anabaptism. Executions and banishments followed in other Swiss cantons as well. In Germany they fared no different. They were persecuted, by both Catholics and Protestants. The aforementioned Second Diet of Speyer in 1529 decreed that all Anabaptists, male or female, of mature age, shall be put to death, by fire, or sword, or otherwise, according to the person, without preceding trial" (Vance, p. 76).

"One citizen who refused to attend sermons was imprisoned, forced to go hear sermons, and finally banished from the city... Calvin used the power of the State to enforce his system of discipline. A hair-dresser was imprisoned for two days for arranging a bride's hair in an unseemly manner. Two Anabaptists were banished from the city on account of their theological views. Penalties were assessed for making a noise or laughing during church. A gambler was publicly punished" (Vance, p. 83).

"The number of dishes eaten at a meal was regulated. Attendance at public worship was made mandatory and watchmen were directed to see that people went to church. Press censorship was instituted and books judged to be heretical or immoral were banned. Interest on loans was capped at 5 percent... during an outbreak of the plague in 1545, over twenty persons were burnt alive for witchcraft, and Calvin himself was involved in the prosecutions. From 1542 to 1546, fifty-eight people were executed and seventy-six exiled from Geneva. Torture was freely used to extract confessions" (Vance, pp. 84-85).

Adulterers and fornicators were imprisoned and fined; they would also be expected to make a public penance (Irwin, pp. 136-137); Calvin favoured the death penalty (Vance, p. 85).

Calvin's own sister-in-law and stepdaughter were both caught in the act of adultery.

"A girl who sang vulgar songs went into exile; a couple whose adultery was uncovered could be publicly disgraced and punished. Originally, this placed too much power in the hands of civil authority. At no moment of the day was the citizen free from the inquisition of public guardians. To make such a system work, spies and informers were needed; and a grosser evil was sometimes introduced in order to chastise a lesser one" (Mumford, p. 189).

John McNeill: "In Calvin's later years, and under his influence, the laws of Geneva became more detailed and more stringent" (McNeill, p. 189).

Schaff reported that, "It is impossible to deny that this kind of legislation savors more of the austerity of old heathen Rome and the Levitical code than of the gospel of Christ, and the actual exercise of discipline was often petty, pedantic and unnecessarily severe" (Schaff, Vol. 8, p. 464).

Lewis Mumford echoes Schaff: "Calvin's Church claimed for itself a more constant supervision over every detail of human life than Rome had claimed. So long as the sinner did not cut himself off from God by heresy, the Catholic Church was lenient to him. But Calvin's government practiced no such indulgence: its aim was to reduce temptation and to root out sin: even little errors in conduct required correction" (Mumford, pp. 189-190).

Nothing in the New Testament writings concerning the New Covenant could ever be used by John Calvin or anybody else to justify the above atrocities. It doesn't matter what age he or others lived in (now or then), this is not the type of behaviour for the Christian to partake in, especially when the Law was fulfilled in Christ – only grace is what should have been practiced in Geneva. And this is something that Caspar Schwenkfeld, I believe, would agree with me on.

I believe Calvin, like all men in positions of power, was fearful of losing his power and grip over the people, so he did whatever was necessary to silence his critics and heretics; and for this, he will be forever tarnished and associated with the class of tyrannical dictators.

In fact, the following Scripture speaks loudly about this type of aggression and brutality: "Then gathered the chief priests and the Pharisees a council, and said, What do we? for this man doeth many miracles. If we let him thus alone, all *men* will believe on him: and the Romans shall come and take away both our place and nation... Then from that day forth they took counsel together for to put him to death" (John 11:47-48, 53).

47

James (or Jacob) Arminius and his Five Points of Arminianism

1) God has decreed to save those who shall believe on Jesus Christ and preserve in faith, leaving the unbelieving in sin, to be condemned.

2) Jesus Christ died for all men, providing redemption if a man believes on him.

3) Man is in a state of sin, unable himself to do anything truly good, but needs to be born again.

4) Man cannot without the grace of God accomplish any good deeds or movements, but this grace can be resisted.

5) Believers have power to persevere, but as to whether they can fall away, that must be more particularly determined out of the Holy Scriptures.

Much to the horror of Calvinists, James Arminius mirrors Calvin in so many ways: both died very young (James at age 49; John at 54). His father died when he was an infant. Calvin lost his mother when only three.

Both were respected scholars and both would end up attacking Rome for her many heretical and man-made doctrines. I suggest they had more in common than many Calvinists are aware or even prepared to publicly acknowledge.

Both Arminius and Calvin were dogged by poor health, for on one occasion, Calvin was housebound for five months, due to a severe illness (De Greef, p. 214). Like Calvin, Arminius suffered numerous physical and theological attacks from his opponents.

For example, both were forced to defend themselves against the charge of Pelagianism (a belief that original sin did not taint human nature, which, being created from God, was divine, and that mortal will is still capable of choosing good or evil without divine aid) (De Greef, p. 162-163).

Both were buried in very modest ways.

Arminius died at home with his family around him whereas Calvin was laid to rest, just a day after he died, in a grave with the initials, "JC," although vandals soon stole it.

Arminius would decline the offer to be a doctor of theology at the University of Basel, would marry and father twelve children, with three dying in infancy, and was incredibly orthodox in his theology, as he accepted the Scriptures to be infallible, believed all 66 books were canonical and accepted the Trinity and the deity of Christ.

Calvinist R.C. Sproul admits that "the language of Augustine, Martin Luther, or John Calvin is scarcely stronger than that of Arminius" (Sproul, *Willing to Believe: The Controversy over Free Will*, p. 126).

Arminius correctly condemned Rome for her many statements that she and she alone could understand and authenticate the Scriptures. He would also line up with Luther in the following attack on the pope: "The adulterer and pimp of the church, the false prophet, the destroyer and subverter of the church, the enemy of God and the Antichrist" (Vance, p. 127).

Luther happily dubbed Leo XIII "your hellishness," but Arminius would go one better: "I openly declare, that I do not own the Roman Pontiff to be a member of Christ's body; but I account him an enemy, a traitor, a sacrilegious and blasphemous man, a tyrant, and a violent usurper of most unjust domination over the church, the man of sin, the son of perdition, that most notorious outlaw" (Vance, p. 127).

"My opinion [on justification] is not so widely different from his [Calvin's] as to prevent me from employing the signature of my own hand in subscribing to those things which he has delivered on this subject, in the third book of his Institutes; this I am prepared to do at any time, and to give them my full approval" (Vance, p. 129).

He would also echo Calvin on the subject of the eternal security of the believer: "At no period have I asserted that believers do finally decline or fall away from faith or salvation" (Vance, p. 130).

He would however "suggest" that it might be possible for a man to fall away from salvation (Arminius, *The Works of James Arminius*, Vol. I, pp. 254-281). Some Calvinists also hold to this too. And I would add that both parties do so because they have failed to rightly divide the word of God into the correct dispensations.

Arminius believed in infant sprinkling. Yet unlike Calvin, this Dutchman never persecuted any of the groups of his day; he would disagree with ones such as the Anabaptists, but always in a Christian framework: Debate them, yes! Harm them, no! Or as the 16th-century lawyer Hugo Grotius put it: "Condemned by others, he condemned none."

The only direct connection between these two Protestant heavyweights would be that Arminius studied at Calvin's Academy, under the watchful eye of Theodore Beza; for Arminius was only four years old when Calvin died.

Arminius was not only tolerant towards Calvin and others, but would highly endorse the writings of Calvin: "I exhort them to read the commentaries of Calvin, on whom I bestow higher praise than Helmichius [a Dutch theologian] ever did, as he confessed to me himself. For I tell them, that his commentaries ought to be held in greater estimation, that all that is delivered to us in the writings of the Ancient Christian Fathers: So that in a certain eminent Spirit of Prophecy, I give the pre-eminence to him beyond most others, indeed beyond them all" (Vance, p. 133).

This remarkable and glowing reference would make any Calvinist blush, for there can be no greater cheerleader than Arminius himself! Yet who can believe such a thing, if one listens to some of the foaming rhetoric from leading Calvinists today and yesteryear?

Well, to top this, I quote one more source, which will astound some: "As to Calvin's extraordinary talents, there can be no doubt. Both in Latin and French, his writings are a model of clear, concise, nervous language; he had great stories of varied learning at his command; his commentaries on Scripture still hold a very high place in the esteem of Protestant scholars, and his subtlety and power of reasoning fitted him to become the great theologian of the Reformed sects. With a vast section of Protestants in Switzerland, Holland, England, Scotland, etc., his Institutes [*Institutio Christianae Religionis*] possessed almost unlimited authority, and were esteemed as the greatest work which had appeared since the days of the Apostles", a quote taken from an official dictionary of the Catholic Church published in 1960 (Addis, p. 98).

Yet the only compliment to be returned to Arminius would have to come from Calvin's successor, Theodore Beza: "Arminius' life and learning have so approved themselves of us… such is our opinion of Arminius – a young man, unquestionably, so far as we are able to judge, most worthy of your kindness and liberality" (Vance, p. 132).

It appears through reading the different accounts of Arminius and Calvin's views that the main issues that caused the split were sin, free will and predestination, something that can either unite or divide a church, even to this day.

Once again, may I quote from the above Catholic dictionary? "Its peculiar doctrines [*Institutes*] have long since lost their hold on Protestants of the better sort, and his system outrages the principles of natural as well of revealed religion" (Addis, p. 98).

Although the doctrine of predestination did not rate very high with Calvin in his first edition of *Institutes*, by the time

Arminius arrived on the scene, this ideology had become a huge issue (even though Luther had not written much about it either).

It's my opinion that some dishonest Calvinists have set out to attack Arminius for no good Scriptural reason whatsoever. So often I've heard the "derogatory" term, "he's an Arminian." Yet if these same Calvinists took the time to read some of Arminius' writings, they would see that they have more in common with him than they do with Augustine!

But regrettably, they have been maligning and misrepresenting Arminius for years!

Louis Berkhof affirmed this: "It is a well known fact that Arminius himself did not depart as far from the Scripture truth and from the teachings of the Reformers as did his followers" (Vance, p. 138).

Other slurs and misrepresentations of Arminius would be how he allegedly held to the doctrine of the "perseverance of the saints." Please see Calvinist Kenneth Good's book on Calvinists which refutes this (Good, *Are Baptists Calvinists?*, p. 63).

The Five Points of Calvinism (TULIP): Total Depravity or Total Inability

"Man is born in sin and is totally dead to the things of God. Until God regenerates those to whom He has personally chosen before the foundation of the world, man remains totally hopeless and has no hope whatsoever of ever being saved from eternal Hell".

The Bible does speak of man's wicked heart and his righteousness being like filthy rags, but to prove total depravity from Scripture is impossible.

"Unregenerate man, therefore, is totally unable to believe or comprehend the things of God until the new birth" (based on 1 Corinthians 2:14).

Again, this is something all faithful believers would have to agree with. Prior to me being saved, the deep things of God were foolishness, but once I was saved, I believed and understood things only a regenerated sinner could.

In Romans 3:10 "There is none righteous, no, not one", Paul quotes Psalm 14 to demonstrate that man has no intention of seeking after God, yet while this may be so, the Calvinist fails to point out Luke 19:10: "For the Son of man is come to seek and to save, that which was lost."

God, therefore, took the initiative and came looking for man, because man wouldn't come looking for Him. And this was something that happened in the Garden of Eden, for God came seeking man; Adam didn't take the initiative to seek out God. All religions of the world have men looking for God. The Bible, on the other hand, has God looking for man.

Yet, while these verses mean what they say, and say what they mean, I believe that the interpretation of such verses is this: in Matthew 19 the Lord was telling the Jews that nobody is as good as God. Nobody lives up to His standard, for we've all missed the mark completely (Psalm 14:3). How true this is!

So, as the Gospel narration goes on, we learn that Jesus would be that perfect Person (Matthew 5:48) that mankind could never be (2 Corinthians 5:21), and in the process Jesus would be the propitiation for sinful mankind and the whole world over (1 John 2:2). With this achieved, man would now be able to have full union and fellowship with a holy and righteous God (1 Timothy 2:5), should he choose to receive Christ as Saviour (John 1:12).

One verse that Calvinists point to for "ammunition" for their belief that the new birth is completely of God, not of men, would be John 1:12-13: "But as many as received him, to them gave he power to become the sons of God, *even* to them that believe on his name: which was born not of blood, nor of the flesh, nor of the will of men, but of God."

Laurence Vance offers the following and simple solution to answer this: "Verse thirteen is giving us the source of the new birth, not the reason why men receive Christ... the new birth is 'not of blood.' The source of the new birth is not reformation, self-development, or self-effort. The new birth is not 'of the will of man.' The source of the new birth is not relatives, preachers, or priests. The threefold negation empathizes the fact that the source of the new birth is of God... the new birth is God's work, but the receiving of Christ is man's" (Vance, p. 217).

Ephesians 1:12-13 also states the believer is saved after hearing the gospel preached: "That we should be to the praise of his glory, who first trusted in Christ. In whom ye also *trusted*, after that ye heard the word of truth, the gospel of your salvation: in whom also after that ye believed, ye were sealed with the holy Spirit of promise."

Therefore, as Romans 10:17 tell us: "faith *cometh* by hearing, and hearing by the word of God."

All men could come to Jesus and follow Him, if they chose to – the Lord tells man to decide which gate to choose to enter (Matthew 7:13) – something that would be absolutely pointless if they were unable to decide for themselves. But they will not (not cannot) come to Jesus because they love their sin too much (John 3:19-21).

"Then Paul and Barnabas waxed bold, and said, It was necessary that the word of God should first have been spoken to you: but seeing ye put it from you [man's own wilful rejection], and judge yourselves unworthy of everlasting life [choose to remain under the powerless Mosaic law], lo, we turn to the Gentiles" (Acts 13:46).

The Bible teaches that man can call on God (Genesis 4:26), reject Him (1 Samuel 8:7), grieve Him (Genesis 6:6), resist

Him (2 Kings 17:13-15), and blaspheme Him (2 Samuel 12:14). It never teaches that man cannot come to Him of his own choice.

It never teaches that man cannot come to Him of his own choice.

Another verse used to try and prove total depravity would be the following: "The wicked, through the pride of his countenance, will not seek *after God*; God *is* not in all his thoughts" (Psalm 10:4). That this verse is speaking of all unsaved and unregenerate people is in no doubt. But let us read carefully what this verse says: "The wicked, through the pride of his countenance, will not seek *after God*." (underlining added). It clearly says that the wicked man will not seek after God, not that he cannot.

This is affirmed in Psalm 119:155: "Salvation *is* far from the wicked: for they seek not thy statutes" (underlining added), and also in the New Testament by the Lord Himself: "Ye will not come to me, that ye might have eternal life" (John 5:40) (underlining added).

Calvinist John MacArthur turns Arminian when he offers the following interpretation of this verse: "They searched for eternal life, but were not willing to trust in its only source" (*The MacArthur Study Bible*, p. 1589).

But one would be justified to ask John MacArthur: "what about irresistible grace???" These verses cannot be used to argue total depravity. Voluntary rejection, yes. Total inability, absolutely not!

It has already been demonstrated above that man has a free will is found and taught in Scripture, so perhaps some more verses need to be offered to convince skeptics: "I make a decree, that all they of the people of Israel, and *of* his priests and Levites, in my realm, which are minded of their own freewill to go up to Jerusalem, go with thee" (Ezra 7:13).

The word freewill appears in Scripture 17 times (1 Chronicles 29:6-9).

Several examples:

– In Leviticus 22:18, God would also call on the Jews to bring their sin offering to Him, with a freewill.

– We also read in Joshua 24:22: "And Joshua said unto the people, Ye *are* witnesses against yourselves that ye have chosen you the LORD, to serve him. And they said, *We are* witnesses."

– Judges 10:14: "Go and cry unto the gods which ye have chosen; let them deliver you in the time of your tribulation."

– 1 Kings 18:21: "And Elijah came unto all the people, and said, How long halt ye between two opinions? if the LORD *be* God, follow him; but if Baal, *then* follow him."

– Manasseh refused to listen to God (2 Chronicles 33:10).

– Hezekiah prayed for Israel saying: "The good LORD pardon everyone *that* prepareth his heart to seek God" (2 Chronicles 30:18-19).

Although Manasseh was a king in God's elect nation, he would commit idolatry, caused his children to pass through fire as living sacrifices to demon gods; used witchcraft and wizards, and defiled the house of God.

So, God raised up the pagan Assyrians to punish him, to bring his elect king back to repentance, who subsequently worked with him going on to cleanse the house of God (2 Chronicles 33:13). And for those that believe a saved party who sins wilfully after receiving the knowledge of the truth can then go on to lose their salvation, clearly this is not the case, for the above king would have been an ideal candidate for such a belief, if not so. While he lost his fellowship with God, he was never in jeopardy of losing his salvation.

Manasseh's two sins of idolatry and child sacrifices both were capital punishments, yet he did not perish. If the truth were known, God loves His people more than we love Him.

In the New Testament, we see that man has a free will and is able to use it when discerning whether or not Jesus came from God (John 7:17).

In Acts 8:37, Scripture demonstrates to the reader how the Ethiopian eunuch, upon believing in Jesus, was asked by Philip: "If thou believest with all thine heart." No coercion from God was used here. The eunuch simply made up his mind, after reading Isaiah 53 and speaking to Philip, used his own free will, and was subsequently baptized once he had believed with all his heart on Jesus.

May I share the following story, taken from Curtis Hutson's 23-page pamphlet: "D. L. Moody addressed a large crowd of skeptics. He said, "I want to talk about the word believe, the word receive, and the word take." "When Mr. Moody had finished his sermon, he asked, 'Now who will come and take Christ as Saviour?' One man stood and said, 'I can't.' Mr Moody wept and said, 'Don't say, 'I can't.' Say, 'I won't! And the man said, 'Then, I won't!' But another man said, 'I will!' Then another said, 'I will!' and another said, 'I will!' Until scores came to trust Christ as Saviour" (Hutson, *Why I Disagree with All Five Points of Calvinism*, p. 5).

While many Calvinists despise the "altar call," Calvinist Gordon Clark said: "Possibly even inviting the audience to walk down to the front could be a good thing" (*Evangelism*, p. 59).

Sproul offers his readers the following: "We may visit the altar many times or respond to invitations." He also went on to say that such calls are able "to strengthen our assurance of salvation and to deepen our commitment to Christ" (Sproul, p. 181).

Calvinist Donald Barnhouse, however, never believed in altar calls. He just preached the gospel and let the Holy Ghost do the work of convicting and drawing sinners to Christ. He did, however, believe regeneration preceded faith!

If we are to believe that Old Testament saints were regenerated by the Lord in order to follow their prophets, and if a person is predestinated and chosen for salvation before the foundation of the world, and if such a person is forever safe in the arms of the Lord, then what are we to make of it when three thousand died due to idolatry and gross immorality (Exodus 32:28)?

The same can be said of Ananias and Sapphira. Both were in the early church, and both sold all they had (voluntarily) and then lied to the Holy Ghost about how much they had received. There is no reason to doubt their salvation, for only a chapter earlier, we note: "And fear came upon every soul: and many wonders and signs were done by the apostles" (Acts 2:43).

Clearly these people must have been regenerated to partake and be in the presence of the Lord? So why didn't they endure to the end of their lives (Matthew 24:13)?

With the Bible advocating free will, not total depravity, it's interesting to note the following Calvinists who agree with this: "[Calvin's] view of the fallen will not only manifest an inconsistency; it is defective as well" (Israel, *The Dutch Republic: Its Rise, Greatness, and Fall 1477-1806*, pp. 425, 440).

Charles Hodge, professor of Princeton University said, "It must, we think, be admitted that to deny the freedom of the will is to take away human responsibility, and therefore human guilt'. There can be no right or wrong, no morality or immorality, if the will is not free. We have no right to punish the criminal for his actions, if he is not a free agent and therefore a responsible agent" (Irwin, pp. 181-182).

"Calvin retains in the fallen state so little of the will as it was created that he cannot explain adequately the moral character of human action in that state, when it still makes choices between good and evil" (Hoitenga, *John Calvin and the Will,* pp. 69-70).

"In this declaration our Lord laid down a principle of supreme practical importance. He informs us how *certainty* may be arrived at in connection with the things of God. He tells us how spiritual discernment and assurance are to be obtained. The fundamental condition for obtaining spiritual *knowledge* is a genuine heart-desire to carry out the revealed will of God in our lives. Wherever the heart is right God gives the capacity to apprehend His truth" (Pink, p. 28).

Peter Ruckman blames Pink for the enormous damage his book *The Sovereignty of God* caused to young street preachers with whom he had personally worked when studying at Bob Jones University. Apparently these men never returned to soul-winning or street work again; they went "slap out of the ministry – permanently" (Ruckman, p. viii).

In David Samuel's book, *The Church in Crisis*, he states: "[churches] are empty because people are no longer drawn to them in their search of God" (Samuel, p. 145). I thought man doesn't seek God on his own merits? Clearly this Calvinist is inconsistent in his own view of irresistible grace!

Like the above quote we find other Calvinists breaking ranks, when a UK Protestant paper *Christian Watch* told an unregenerate man to "believe upon Christ with the whole heart." So, it's interesting that some Calvinists don't hold completely to the first part of the TULIP!

However, other Calvinists make their views very clear on this: "Freewill is the invention of man, instigated by the devil"

(Wilmoth, *The Baptist Examiner*, p. 5).

"The heresy of freewill dethrones God and enthrones man" (Best, *Free Grace Versus Free Will*, p. 35).

Because Calvinists believe that "dead men" cannot believe on Christ unless God draws them and regenerates them first, then it would be logical to say that "dead men" cannot disbelieve Christ either.

In my discussions with Calvinists over the years, the one thing that comes through time and time again is that God must receive all the glory for man's salvation. This I would agree with totally. But like everything else with Calvinism, what they mean is that man has no part whatsoever in responding to the gospel. To the Calvinist, man is no more than a robot or a meaningless puppet waiting to be programmed to believe in/on Jesus Christ, and unless the Operator does this programming, then the robot is forever shut down and totally oblivious to the dire need of repentance and the new birth, something Calvinists omit to inform their audience, for God has already granted repentance to the Jews (Acts 5:31), and the Gentiles (Acts 11:18).

(More on this later).

Unconditional Election

"Not all men are created with similar destiny but eternal life is foreordained for some, and eternal damnation for others. Every man, therefore, being created for one or the other of these ends, we say, he is predestinated to life or to death" (Calvin, *Institutes*, Book III, chapter 23).

The Westminster Confession of Faith and the Canons of Dort later affirmed Calvin's doctrine: "By the decree of God, for the manifestation of His own glory, some men and angels are predestinated unto everlasting life, and others foreordained to everlasting death."

Sproul sadly held to this view (Sproul, p. 22).

Calvinists believe it is God's good pleasure to damn billions to Hell. However, the Scripture doesn't teach this, but quite the opposite: "Say unto them, *As* I live, saith the Lord GOD, I have no pleasure in the death of the wicked; but that the wicked turn from his way and live: turn ye, turn ye from your evil ways; for why will ye die, O house of Israel?" (Ezekiel 33:11).

Billton has the following words of condemnation to this: "God does not love everybody; in fact He hates most people, because they are not elected, and is going to condemn them to hell for ever, and there is nothing the sinful unelected can do... And they have the audacity to call that 'The Gospel,' Good News for sinners" (Billton, p. 114).

So, not only do Calvinists contradict one another, but more

importantly, Calvinism contradicts Scripture; for God takes no pleasure in wicked people perishing, but He wants to be reconciled to man. Again, this is something that the New Testament speaks of: "Now then we are ambassadors for Christ, as though God did beseech *you* by us: we pray *you* in Christ's stead, be ye reconciled to God" (2 Corinthians 5:20).

"For the love of Christ constraineth us; because we thus judge, that if one died for all, then were all dead: And that he died for all, that they which live should not henceforth live unto themselves, but unto him which died for them, and rose again" (2 Corinthians 5:14-15).

Here we read how the Saviour died for all, for all are dead in sin, elect and non-elect included. Then we read the following: "God was in Christ, reconciling the world unto himself, not imputing their trespasses unto them; and hath committed unto us the word of reconciliation" (2 Corinthians 5:19). Now, this verse does not teach the heresy of universalism, but what it does clearly teach is that God has provided an atonement for the world over.

(More on this under "Limited Atonement")

What about those who don't believe on Jesus?

"For I could wish that myself were accursed from Christ for my brethren, my kinsmen according to the flesh" (Romans 9:3).

What a strange thing for Paul to say when, according to the Canons of Dort, God never willed it to save the billions that go to Hell in the first place. God only intended to save a limited number. One would think that a man who was raptured to the third Heaven would know this so-called "Christian belief"? Perhaps the Calvinists should explain to Paul that it is God's *good pleasure to ordain the majority to Hell, and the few to Heaven.*

With the vast majority of Calvinists upholding the above confession of faith, it is interesting to note what the following Calvinists have to say about this second part of the TULIP: "Predestination occupies a comparatively small place in Calvin's teachings... the subject of predestination occupies four chapters out of eighty, or fifty pages out of two volumes of 1,200 pages, one twenty-fourth part of the whole" (Irwin, p. 174).

"The doctrine [predestination] is not mentioned in the first edition of the *Institutes*. He mentions it first in the edition of 1539 and then only in passing. It assumes prominence in later editions" (Bratt, p. 49).

Calvin taught some were chosen to life; some were chosen to damnation (Irwin, p. 61). He would say: "All are not created on equal terms, but some are preordained to eternal life, others to eternal damnation; and accordingly as each has been created for one or others of these ends, we say that he has been predestinated to life or to death" (Bilton, p. 101). Calvin would go on to say: "I admit it is dreadful" (Irwin, p. 62).

Billton offers the following to this type of twisted Scriptural tampering: "God hates most people and has appointed them to damnation...what a monster of a God they depict in their theology" (Bilton, p. 9).

Calvin believed, much to the disagreement of today's Calvinists, that Romans 9 was speaking about nations, not individuals (Irwin, p. 63).

The following quote comes from Heinrich Bullinger: "Believe me, many are displeased with what you say in your Institutes about predestination" (Schaff, Vol. 8, p. 618).

Out of Spurgeon's one thousand sermons, only ten contained the doctrine and preaching of TULIP.

Yet when Calvin was pressed to defend this position, he said: "No one will ever attempt to disprove the doctrine which I have set forth herein, but he who may imagine himself to be wiser than the Spirit of God" (Calvin, *Eternal Predestination*, p. 185). Such a bizarre and prideful statement as this sounds to me like Calvin was once again offering himself and his "writings" to be on par with Scripture. A very dangerous and deranged thing to do!

Did God create evil and is He the author of sin?

"God, from all eternity, did by the most wise and holy counsel of His own will,

freely, and unchangeably ordain whatsoever comes to pass: yet so, as thereby neither is God the author of sin, nor is violence offered to the will of the creatures; nor is the liberty or contingency of second causes taken away, but rather established" (Sproul, p. 28).

However, Jean Trolliet (one of Geneva's notaries) believed Calvin and his writings taught that God was the author of sin. So enraged by this "slur," the following statement was put out from city officials, in defence of Calvin's *Institutes*: "Calvin's book of the Institutes was a good and godly composition... no one should dare to speak against this book and its doctrine" (*Register of Geneva*, p. 201).

Arminius also believed Calvin made the Lord the author of sin! (Vance, p. 133).

Ruckman too: "It is more than evident that this [Psalm 115:3; Proverbs 16:9] includes all the actions of men [rape, child molesting, cursing, lying, swearing, cheating, torturing, sex perversion, blackmail, embezzlement, etc] and this truth is more clearly seen in special instances. Many... refer all these statements to the permissive will of God (rape, child molesting, cursing, lying, swearing, cheating, etc). But this solution appears to me unwise. His will (God's) is one and undivided"

(Ruckman, p. 23).

This book has thus far exposed the legalism, the self-proclaimed "theocracy," and the killing of those who refused to bow the knee to this Genevan and his cruel council. Such charges as these are most profound, and the repercussions for the Reformed world for those that follow him will no doubt be deafening. However, if these things weren't serious enough, there is one sin that Billton believes Calvin to be guilty of. A sin so serious, that if it were true, then this man is forever lost in Hell. Yes, the unpardonable sin!

Perhaps I had better quote Billton one last time and let him explain his position: "In Matthew 12:24, the Pharisees accused the Lord Jesus of casting out demons by Beelzebub and by so doing they were committing the unpardonable sin, by attributing to Satan the work of the Spirit of God through Jesus, as Jesus tells them in Verse 31. Surely Augustine and Calvin are doing the same, by attributing the evil deeds of men and the work of Satan, to the work of God's Spirit"? (Billton, p. 246).

I am not necessarily saying that Calvin was lost or committed the unpardonable sin, for even Ruckman suggested elsewhere how Calvin *might have been saved*, although he calls him a "wretch of a man." All I am doing is presenting the thoughts and comments from those in Calvin's camp and those outside. I will leave you, the reader, to check these statements and come to your own conclusion. However, Calvin would contradict what he just said and would say it was blasphemy to identify God as the author of sin. Yet, he later would say that what he teaches does not come out of his own head; he has received it from God" (Guinness, *Romanism and the Reformation*, p. 52).

It would appear once again that Calvin was claiming "divine inspiration" for his "writings," something only the writers of the Bible are credited for (2 Peter 1:21).

"Not only did His omniscient eye see Adam eating of the forbidden fruit, but He decreed beforehand that he should do so" (Pink, *The Sovereignty of God*, p. 249).

Incidentally, Pink, who was saved in his bedroom as a youth, dropped out of the Moody Bible Institute after spending just six weeks there as a student and also went on to abandon his pre-millennial beliefs. Years later, after failing to find a church to pastor in America, Britain, and Australia, he became a recluse, along with his wife, Vera. They produced a newsletter, which was read by a very small circle of people and in reality, they cut themselves off from the wider world. He died in the Scottish Hebrides, apparently unnoticed by the world. (Couch, *Dictionary of Premillennial Theology*, p. 306).

A Calvinist professor from Germany, John Piscator, stated that, "God justly wills that sins be committed by us, and indeed absolutely wills that they be committed; nay, procures in time these sins themselves" (Vance, p. 254).

"God eternally hates some men; has immutably decreed their damnation; and has determined to withhold them from Christ, grace, faith, and salvation" (Engelsma, *Hyper-Calvinism and the Call of the Gospel: An Examination of the Well-Meant Gospel Offer*, p. 45).

Lorraine Boettner: "It is hard for us to realize that many of those around us (in some cases our close friends and relatives) are probably foreordained to eternal punishment" (Boettner, *Predestination*, p. 125). And yet Boettner would "tempt fate" by saying: "Prove any one of them false and the whole system must be abandoned" (Boettner, p. 5).

This smug and arrogant hymn is an old Baptist one. Yet isn't pride condemned in Scripture? (Proverbs 8:13).

"We are the Lord's elected few,

Let all the rest be damned;

There's room enough in hell for you,

We won't have heaven crammed"! (Vance, p. 300).

Such statements and views as this make God out to be some kind of a monster, which is exactly what Arno Gaebelein said when he broke fellowship with Arthur Pink over his book *The Sovereignty of God*: "It is just this kind of teaching which makes atheists" (Vance, p. 290).

These hyper-Calvinistic views (supralapsarianism) were once held by Calvin himself, yet according to the Calvinist Arthur Custance, in Calvin's latter years, he "softened his position" (Custance, *The Sovereignty of God*, pp. 159-160).

There are other Calvinists who cause divisions in their ranks:

Beza: "God himself is neither the author of sin nor a participant in the act of sinning" (Muller, *Christ and the*

Decree, p. 84).

Sproul: "One thing is absolutely unthinkable, that God could be the author or doer of sin" (Sproul, p. 31).

More Calvinists come to the aid of Beza and Sproul: "[It is] illogical, ridiculous, nonsensical, and foolish" (Palmer, *The Five Points of Calvinism*, p. 85).

"God does not create men in order to destroy them" (Hodge, *Romans*, p. 321).

Those of the last one hundred years or so who would agree with Beza, Muller, and Palmer on this one point would be D. L. Moody, Billy Sunday, and J. Vernon McGee, just to list a few!

Yet in the times of the Reformation, it fell to the Wesley brothers and James Arminius to respond to this poisoned chalice, and refute it. And we mustn't forget to mention King James I who had the following to say of this: "This doctrine is so horrible, that I am persuaded, if there were a council of unclean spirits assembled in hell, and their prince the devil were to put the question either to all of them in general, or to each in particular, to learn their opinion about the most likely means of stirring up the hatred of men against God their Maker; nothing could be invented by them that would be more efficacious for this purpose, or that could put a greater affront upon God's love for mankind, than that infamous decree of the late Synod [of Dort], and the decision of that detestable formulary, by which the far greater part of the human race are condemned to hell for no other reason, *than the mere will of God, without any regard to sin*; the necessity of sinning, as well as that of being damned, being fastened on them by that great nail of the decree before-mentioned" (Arminius, Vol. I, p. 213).

John Wesley condemns this by saying: "Sing, O hell, and rejoice ye that are under the earth. For God, even the mighty God, hath spoken and doomed to death thousands of souls, from the rising of the sun to the going down thereof. Here, O death, is thy sting. They shall not, cannot escape. For the mouth of the Lord hath spoken. Here, O grave, is thy victory. Nations yet unborn, or even they have done good or evil, are doomed never to see the light of life, but thou shalt gnaw upon them for ever and ever. Let all those morning stars sing together who fell with Lucifer, sun of the morning. Let all the sons of hell shout for joy. For the decree is past and who shall disannul it" (Vance, p. 293).

Calvin: "I freely acknowledge my doctrine to be this: that Adam fell, not only by the permission of God, but by His very secret council and decree; and that Adam drew all his posterity with himself, by his fall, into eternal damnation" (Calvin, *Secret Providence*, p. 267).

Because many Calvinists refuse to hold to man's freewill, it shouldn't come as a surprise that there are Calvinists that reject praying, for God has already decreed the end from the beginning.

David S. West stated that, "Prayer does not change things, nor does prayer change God or His Mind" (*The Baptist Examiner*, 18/2/89, p. 5).

Even Martin Lloyd-Jones had a similar and peculiar view: "My friend, if you are a Christian, do you know that you were the object of God's interest and concern before the foundation of the world? All these things have been worked out in eternity, before time, so you must always remember that nothing can happen in time which will make the slightest difference" (Lloyd-Jones, *Saved in Eternity: The Assurance of Our Salvation*, p. 16).

So, with the above clearly in mind, we can fully sympathise with Billton's understanding of just how harsh and desperate Calvinism is: "If you are saved don't bother to pray for your lost ones, because if they are not among the elect, you can pray as earnestly as you like, they won't be saved if God hates them, and if they are elected they will be saved anyway" (Billton, p. 114).

I chose you!

John 15:16 is one of several key verses which Calvinists use to try and prove their theory of God choosing those whom He will before the world began: "Ye have not chosen me, but I have chosen you, and ordained you, that ye should go and bring forth fruit, and *that* your fruit should remain: that whatsoever ye shall ask of the Father in my name, he may give it you."

The verse is clearly speaking about Jesus choosing His apostles for service, not to save them from Hell. Once saved, fruit would come from their new lives. But we must also remember that the Lord Jesus did not choose these twelve men before the world began, but while He was here on the earth, and Luke tells us He prayed all night before He was sure whom He wanted

(Luke 6:12).

Please also remember that Luke 10 tells us that there were many other disciples that followed the Lord, and any one of them could have been chosen too. We also read from John 6 that many chose to reject Him of their own free will.

Romans 9 is also cited by Calvinists to prove their doctrine that God, in eternity past, chose some for Heaven and chose others for Hell. However, not all Calvinists believe this to be so. Herman Ridderbos stated that this chapter spoke of "the principle that God's election is not of works and that the destiny of Israel as a whole is in view" (Vance, p. 323).

Calvinist Oliver Buswell, former president of Wheaton College, would also take issue with his fellow Calvinists' stock interpretation of Romans 9, for he would say: "In the Malachi passage from which Paul quotes these words, the prophet is clearly referring not to individual Esau, but to the people of Edom who had been a sinful and rebellious people, though they were, according to the promises of God, eligible to be considered within God's covenant with Israel. There is nothing in the Genesis record to indicate that Esau, when Jacob returned to his home land, was other than a sincere worshiper" (Buswell, *A Systematic Theology of the Christian Religion*, Vol. 2, p. 148).

L.S. Ballard would also contribute on this passage: "To contend that this election was to salvation is preposterous, false, and as far from the truth as heaven is to hell, or as the east is from the west. It was an election to national preference or theocratic privileges and there is nothing akin to salvation in it" (Ballard, *Election Made Plain*, p. 15).

Ruckman has the following to offer: "Two nations in thy womb." There weren't two literal nations inside of Rebekah. Obviously the statement is figurative. Esau represents one nation, and Jacob represents another nation. It is a statement of prophecy based on God's knowledge of the future. Look at verse 13. Verse 13 is a quote from Malachi 1:2-3 where God is looking back over His dealings with Edom and Israel. It had nothing to do with the individual salvation of Jacob or the individual damnation of Esau" (Ruckman, *The Book of Romans*, p. 354).

Acts 13:48-49 is used by the Calvinists to demonstrate again their view of people being chosen before the world: "And when the Gentiles heard this, they were glad, and glorified the word of the Lord: and as many as were ordained to eternal life believed. And the word of the Lord was published throughout all the region."

John MacArthur called this passage: "One of Scripture's clearest statements on the sovereignty of God in salvation. God chooses man for salvation, not the opposite" (MacArthur, *Study Bible*, p. 1658).

However, Oliver Buswell once again differs from his Calvinist colleague: "Actually the words of Acts 13:48-49, do not necessarily have any reference whatsoever to the doctrine of God's eternal decree of election" (Buswell, Vol. 2, p. 152).

Is not this verse simply referring to the fact that all are ordained to everlasting life ("And I, if I be lifted up from the earth, will draw all *men* unto me", John 12:32), but only those that actually believe and receive Christ are then appointed to receive life eternal ("But as many as received him, to them gave he power to become the sons of God, *even* to them that believe on his name" John 1:12)?

If the elect are elected unconditionally, then how are we to understand 1 Corinthians 1:26? "For ye see your calling, brethren, how that not many wise men after the flesh, not many mighty, not many noble *are called*." This verse would seem to teach that God's election was conditional, for He chose the base sort to be saved (vs. 28), and not the high flyers and wealthy which, I must say, most well-known Calvinists are!

I once told a Presbyterian Calvinist that he couldn't go to Hell even if he wanted to. "Either you're saved or you're not," I said. He looked very upset and shocked at this. Yet Calvinists believe that if they are one of the elect, then they couldn't be lost even if they wanted to (Vance, p. 386). Or as Arthur Custance put it: "No man elected to salvation could possibly die or be killed unsaved" (Custance, p. 24).

We must also remember that Calvinists believe all the elect are in chosen in Christ before the world began. However, this philosophy of the French reformer is foreign to Scripture, for in Romans 16:7, Andronicus and Junia were "in Christ" before Paul.

And in John's Gospel 17:6, we read that the ones given to Jesus were men. Women and children, it would seem, weren't called?!?

Eleven chapters earlier, Jesus told the multitude: "Labour not for the meat that perisheth, but for the meat which endureth unto everlasting life, which the Son of man shall give unto you: for him hath God the Father sealed" (John 6:27).

Yet by verse 36, we read: "But I said unto you, That ye also have seen me, and believe not." And in verse 66, we read: "From that *time* many of his disciples went back, and walked no more with him."

So, if all these people were regenerated and offered eternal life (vs. 27) – for according to the Calvinist doctrine, God only gives eternal life to His chosen elect before the world was – how are we to understand many rejecting His irresistible grace and leaving Him indefinitely?

It is clear, therefore, that God holds man accountable for his decision as to whether or not to receive or reject Christ because man is fully capable of deciding which route he wishes to take in the first place. And also why would Christ have spent over three and a half years crisscrossing Israel offering everlasting life to people that a) He knew would not receive it, and b) He knew could not receive it? To suggest that Jesus wasn't really sincere in His call to repentance is blasphemous, and seeks only to dishonour His genuine and authentic desire to see all of His audience believe on Him.

Can God's decrees be overthrown or changed by man?

Such a question as this will no doubt seem preposterous to many Calvinists, yet what does the Bible say on this?

Two decrees are worth mentioning. This first: "Then said David, Will the men of Keilah deliver me and my men into the hand of Saul? And the LORD said, They will deliver *thee* up" (1 Samuel 23:12).

This didn't happen and it didn't happen for one reason: David left the city of his own freewill, thus avoiding what would have happened had he stayed.

The second is Jonah and the people of Nineveh: "And Jonah began to enter into the city a day's journey, and he cried, and said, Yet forty days, and Nineveh shall be overthrown. So the people of Nineveh believed God, and proclaimed a fast, and put on sackcloth, from the greatest of them even to the least of them" (Jonah 3:4-5).

Again, man was able to avoid the consequences of God's decree by taking heed to His warning, via His prophet Jonah.

One other segment of Holy Writ should be cited to demonstrate how God could decree something, man refuses it, and subsequently punishment from God/man follows.

Let the reader also be reminded that Israel is God's elect: "Then the LORD said unto me, Proclaim all these words in the cities of Judah, and in the streets of Jerusalem, saying, Hear ye the words of this covenant, and do them. For I earnestly protested unto your fathers in the day *that* I brought them up out of the land of Egypt, *even* unto this day, rising early and protesting, saying, Obey my voice. Yet they obeyed not, nor inclined their ear, but walked every one in the imagination of their evil heart: therefore I will bring upon them all the words of this covenant, which I commanded *them* to do; but they did *them* not" (Jeremiah 11:6).

The New Testament also has decrees which God gives, but once again, they are conditional upon you responding to it: "But the Pharisees and lawyers rejected the council of God against themselves, being not baptized of him" (Luke 7:30).

"For this *is* good and acceptable in the sight of God our Saviour; Who will have all men to be saved, and to come unto the knowledge of the truth" (1 Timothy 2:3-4).

Infant 'salvation'

It might infuriate some to learn that there are Calvinists (including Calvin himself) that believe that dead babies who aren't baptized go to Hell upon death.

In the Catholic Church, when the priest baptizes the child, this not only "washes away original sin, but apparently also exorcises any demonic spirits. That's right! The priest performs an exorcism on your child! Nurses and nuns working in Catholic hospitals sprinkle dying infants, even without the consent and knowledge of their parents. For years, the Catholic Church even practiced this among its laity. Isn't it tragic how the Reformers didn't ditch this blasphemous view?

Like Augustine, Calvin held to the view that some non-baptized dead infants would suffer eternal damnation (Schaff, Vol. 8, pp. 558-559).

No wonder the former Prime Minister Gordon Brown and his wife urgently sent for a minister of the Church of Scotland to baptize their dying daughter, when only ten days old. Mr Brown obviously still holds to his late father's Calvinistic beliefs.

So incensed was Charles Wesley with this appalling and heretical view that he put pen to paper and came up with the following:

"God, ever merciful and just,

With newborn babes did Tophet fill;

Down into endless torments thrust;

Merely to show His sovereign will.

This is "Horrible Decree"!

This is that wisdom from beneath!

God (O detest the Blasphemy)

Hath pleasure in the sinners' death" (Vance, p. 399).

For once at least, Wesley would have been utterly surprised, as Spurgeon concurred with his opponent's view on this Catholic practice: "A human and carnal invention, an addition to the word of God, and therefore wicked and injurious... There is no distinction between a child of godly or ungodly parents" (Spurgeon, *Infant Salvation*, p. 3, 35).

Ruckman offers his thoughts to this blasphemous babble: "Do you honestly think that the Lord who said, 'Suffer the little children to come unto me, and forbid them not' (Mark 10:14), would send a little baby who didn't even know the difference between right and wrong or good and evil to Hell or some place away from Him, like Limbo? You're crazy" (Ruckman, *The Book of Romans*, p. 163).

In John MacArthur's book *Safe in the Arms of God* he recalls an occasion when he was part of a panel of theologians asked where dead infants go when they die. After asking four out of the five members, and with each one answering they didn't know, he was the first one to respond emphatically that they were safe in the arms of God, whether they had been baptized or not, regardless of their parents' faith or non-faith in Jesus.

Charles Spurgeon would also have concurred with MacArthur, for he would say: "Among the gross falsehoods which have been uttered against the Calvinists proper, is the wicked calumny that we hold the damnation of little infants. A baser lie was never uttered. There may have existed somewhere, in some corner of the earth, a miscreant who would dare say there were infants in hell, but I have never met with him, nor have I met with a man who ever saw such a person" (Spurgeon, *The Doctrines of Grace*, p. 300).

With these two Calvinists agreeing that dead infants would be elect, and with Spurgeon's words: "I have never met with him, nor have I met with a man who ever saw such a person," he should have recalled how Augustine and Calvin were such men. For both believed in the damnation of all non-baptized infants (Schaff, Vol. 8, pp. 558-559).

Out of all the reformers, however, Zwingli was the only who held to universal salvation for dead infants.

Luther, on the other hand, seemed to be unable to publicly commit himself to go on record and tell his congregation how Zwingli was correct; for he feared his church members would not bother to bring their children forward to be baptized in future and, therefore, church earnings would go down (George, *Theology of the Reformers*, p. 95).

The Scriptures that MacArthur's colleagues should have cited to prove salvation for all dead infants would be Deuteronomy 1:39 and Romans 4:15 and 5:13:

– "Moreover your little ones, which ye said should be a prey, and your children, which in that day had no knowledge between good and evil, they shall go in thither, and unto them will I give it, and they shall possess it" (Deuteronomy 1:39)

– "Because the law worketh wrath: for where no law is, *there is* no transgression" (Romans 4:15)

– "For until the law sin was in the world: but sin is not imputed when there is no law" (Romans 5:13)

Hutson's opinion was: "The doctrine that God elected some men to Hell, that they were born to be damned by God's own choice, is a radical heresy not taught anywhere in the Bible" (Hutson, p. 7).

Limited Atonement

"If they [Arminians] could prove that the love which prompted God to give his son to die, as a sin-offering, on the cross, had for its objects all men indiscriminately, and that Christ actually sacrificed his life with the purpose of saving all indifferently on the condition of faith, then it appears that their inference is irresistible that the central principle of Arminianism is true" (Hodge, *The Atonement*, p. 348).

Confusion seems to abound as to whether or not Calvin held to an atonement for the elect of God only, or for the whole of creation. I am convinced that Beza held to a limited atonement, but whether or not Calvin did, remains unclear amongst some Calvinists.

"There is too little evidence in the Institutes to reach a conclusion on the extent of the atonement" (Peterson, *Calvin's Doctrine of the Atonement*, p. 90).

So, I have decided to list two of his commentaries on the atonement, which I believe suggest that Calvin held to unlimited atonement:

On the subject of 1 Timothy 3: "We say what everyone sees: It is God's will that we should all be saved, when He commands that His Gospel should be preached... We ought, therefore, as far as lies in our power, to seek the salvation of those who are to-day strangers to the faith, and endeavour to bring them to the goodness of God. And why? Because Jesus Christ is not the Saviour of three or four, but offers Himself to all... Jesus

Christ did not come to be mediator between two or three men, but between God and men; not to reconcile a small number of people to God, but to extend His grace to the whole world" (Irwin, pp. 180-181).

On 1 John 2:2: "Christ suffered for the sins of the whole world, and in the goodness of God is offered unto all men without distinction, his human blood being shed not for a part of the world only, but for the whole human race; for although in the world nothing is found worthy of the favour of God, yet he holds out the propitiation to the whole world, since without exception he summons all to the faith in Christ, which is nothing than the door unto hope" (Strong, p. 778).

This view of unlimited atonement is affirmed by Calvinist James Richards, who stated that Calvin re-examined limited atonement as he got older and came to an understanding of unlimited atonement (Richards, *Lectures on Mental Philosophy and Theology*, p. 308).

If one takes the time to read *The Articles of Faith* for the Church of England, published after Calvin died, we discover that the Anglican Church (Article 31) also held to an unlimited atonement: "...the offering of Christ once made is the perfect redemption, propitiation, and satisfaction, for all sinnes of the whole worlde" (Schaff, *Creeds*, Vol. 3, p. 507).

Luther, in his commentary on Galatians, said the following: "One that hath taken upon Him the sins of all men... By this means the whole world is purged" (Samuel, p. 89) (underlining added).

The five-point Calvinist Bob Ross, dubbed by Eddie Garrett as "an Arminian posing as a Calvinist," said: "All those that want to be saved will be," therefore the blood of Christ would have to be capable to cleanse all sinners of the world (Revelation 1:5).

However, the problem Calvinists have with the blood of Christ is this: if He died for all, then His blood was wasted, for most will perish. Unfortunately, man with his limited understanding of the atonement approaches this subject without being able to fathom how God distributes the blood to repentant sinners.

Robert Dabney hits the nail right on the head: "Had every sinner of Adam's race been elected, the same one sacrifice would be sufficient for all. We must absolutely get rid of the mistake that expiation is an aggregate of gifts to be divided and distributed out, one piece to each receive" (Dabney, *The Five Points of Calvinism*, p. 61).

Please see two totally opposite views, taken from two Calvinist writers: "A Christ for all is really a Christ for none" (Hoeksema, *Limited Atonement*, p. 65).

"Christ died for the whole created world (John 3:16) including Satan" (North, *Dominion and Common Grace*, p. 43).

For whom did Christ die?

– Jesus loved His own until the end (John 13:1)

– He laid His life down for His friends (John 15:13), which were publicans and sinners (Luke 7:34)

– He called Judas His friend (Matt. 26:50).

– He chose Judas (the same Greek word for 'chose' is *eklego* and is also used in Ephesians 1:4).

– He prophetically called Judas mine own familiar friend (Psalm 41:9).

– He died for false prophets by buying them with His own precious blood; hence, how they were able to go on to deny Him (2 Peter 2:1).

> – He died for all of nature. His crown of thorns (Matthew 27:29) would be a fulfillment of Genesis 3:18, where He paid for the sins of all nature; this is pictured in Isaiah 11:6 and Romans 8:22. Matthew 13:44 would also be a picture of Jesus buying the field (the whole world, vs. 38) with His own blood.

– Through the atonement, God has made possible the provision for all mankind, but mankind must accept the appropriation if salvation is to be of any benefit (Matthew 11:28).

And for once, even Augustine got this one point right:

"Christ's blood is sufficient for all, but it is only efficient for those who seek it."

But Dr. Paul Reiter, still unsure about this, asks the question: "For whom did the Saviour die"?

Well, the Bible tells us He died for:

– All men (1 Timothy 2:6; Isaiah 53:6)

– For every man (Hebrew 2:9)

– For the world (John 3:16)

– For the sins of the whole world (1 John 2:2)

– For false teachers that deny Him (2 Peter 2:1)

– For many (Matthew 20:28)

– For Israel (John 11:50-51)

– For the Church (Ephesians 5:25)

– And for me (Galatians 2:20)

And if the above Scriptures aren't clear enough, may I quote Richard Baxter: "Now I would know of any man, would you believe that Christ died for all men if the Scripture plainly speak it? If you would, do but tell me, what words can you devise or would you wish more plain for it than are there used? Is it not enough that Christ is called the Saviour of the World? You'll say, but is it of the whole world? Yes, it saith, He is the propitiation for the sins of the whole World. Will you say, but it is not for All men in the World? Yes it saith he died for

All men, as well as for all the World. But will you say, it saith not for every man? Yes it doth say, he tasted death for every man. But you may say, It means all the Elect, if it said so of any Non-Elect I would believe. Yes, it speaks of those that denied the Lord that bought them, and bring upon themselves swift destruction. And yet all this seems nothing to men prejudiced."

Therefore the Bible clearly and unambiguously states the following (underlining added):

"God was in Christ, reconciling the world unto himself [provision]...we pray *you* in Christ's stead, be ye reconciled to God" [appropriation] (2 Corinthians 5:19-20).

"Who is the Saviour of all men [provision], specially of those that believe [appropriation]" (1 Timothy 4:10.)

"Who gave himself a ransom for all, to be testified in due time" (1 Timothy 2:6).

"Therefore as by the offence of one [Adam] *judgment came* upon all men to condemnation [everyone has the problem of original sin]; even so by the righteousness of one [Jesus] *the free gift came* upon all men unto justification of life [provision for all of mankind without exception but only of benefit to those that personally appropriate/receive this gift]. For as by one man's disobedience many [used interchangeably with all from above] were made sinners [without exception], so by the obedience of one shall many [again used interchangeably with all from above] be made righteous" (Romans 5:18-19).

He would taste death for every man (Hebrews 2:9).

Not once, not twice, but often Jesus called Jerusalem to come to Him (Matthew 23:37).

Why would Jesus bother to do this if a) He didn't really mean it and b) He knew they couldn't anyway?

"For God so loved the world, that he gave his only begotten son [provision], that whosoever believeth in him [appropriation] should not perish, but have everlasting life" (John 3:16).

"Behold I stand at the door, and knock [provision]: if any man hear my voice, and open the door [appropriation], I will come into him, and will sup with him, and he with me" (Revelation 3:20).

It should be pointed out again that when the Bible uses the word "many" or "all" most of the time both words are used interchangeably, for example:

Mark 1:32-34: All came to be healed by Him. He healed many of them.

Matthew 8:16: Many were brought to Him. He healed all who were sick.

Whilst leading Calvinists hold to the view of a limited atonement, what is intriguing is how MacArthur, who also holds to this view, "unfortunately" contradicts himself when he says the following of Jesus: "...becoming an atonement for the sins of the very ones who killed Him" (MacArthur, *The Murder of Jesus*, p. XIV).

The ones who killed Him (e.g., Caiaphas, Pilate, and Herod)

never repented and believed on Him, so MacArthur will have to re-evaluate his private interpretation on this. Either Christ died for the elect only, or He didn't. With all of the above dying in their sins, MacArthur will have to decide if they were indeed never members of the elect or if Jesus' precious blood was wasted for them, for he can't have it both ways!

Sir Robert Anderson had the following to say about his struggle with false "tradition" and his presuppositions when reading the Bible: "In the early years of my Christian life I was greatly perplexed and distressed by the supposition that the plan and simple words of Scriptures as John 3:16; 1 John 2:2; 1 Timothy 2:6 were not true, save in a cryptic sense understood only by the initiated. For, I was told, the over-shadowing truth of Divine sovereignty in election barred our taking them literally. But half a century ago a friend of those days-the late Dr. Horatius Bonar-delivered me from this strange prevalent error. He taught me that truths may seem to us irreconcilable only because our finite minds cannot understand the Infinite; and we must never allow our faulty apprehension of the eternal counsels of God to hinder unquestioning faith in the words of Holy Scripture."

Does this sound a little familiar to you? Where else have we heard this type of battle before? Yes, that's right, evolution!

Sir Fred Hoyle: "As a young student I was brainwashed into accounting everything without God."

Praise the Lord! Hoyle saw through the lie and deceit of evolution, and so too did Anderson with the vain philosophy of Calvinism!

Irresistible Grace

"Grace means 'God's unmerited favour.' Or G-R-A-C-E means God's riches at Christ's expense" (Hutson, p. 13).

There are two verses that have been argued over and debated more than most and they are 1 Timothy 2:4; 2 Peter 3:9.

Paul, it seems, teaches that God's will is for all men to be saved. So strong is this interpretation that even the leading apologist Lorraine Boettner sees how this view can be taken.

The question as always must be this: Does God want all men to be saved or not? According to Calvinist John Piper: [He] "desires the salvation of all men" (Piper, *Are There Two Wills in God?*", 1 January 1995.

Yet Piper, I believe, is a solemn voice in the community of Calvinism.

According to the Lord Jesus, the Holy Spirit would reprove the world of sin, yet according to Calvinists, this would not only be unnecessary but contrary to the TULIP. For if God will only save the elect, and if Jesus' blood is only efficient for this group, why then would the Holy Ghost need to convict the whole world of sin, if it can't benefit them?

Charles Wesley: "O horrible decree, worthy of whence it came! Forgive their hellish blasphemy who charge it to the Lamb"! (Schaff, Vol. 8, p. 567).

If Protestants are content to challenge the pope to release all souls from purgatory, something Rome teaches he can do whenever he so desires, then these same Protestants, one would think, might hold to the belief that if God uses *irresistible grace* to woo ungodly depraved sinners to salvation, then why not use irresistible grace on all? If the pope is challenged to release all tormented souls from the excruciating pain of purgatory, then why doesn't God inflict His irresistible grace upon all?

The papacy doesn't have the power to release anybody from purgatory, for there is no purgatory, and the Lord is near to all those that will call on Him (Psalm 145:18); but man loves his sin, which grieves the Lord (Ezekiel 6:9).

This dreadful doctrine of Calvinism must be Biblically sound, if it is to be trusted and relied upon as orthodox theology. But as we have already seen, when the Reformers go to men such as Augustine, then one is truly heading for theological suicide, not to mention genocide!

When does repentance come to the sinner?

The late Donald Barnhouse, another five-point Calvinist, told his radio audience that regeneration and repentance would have to come to the sinner before he/she could believe on Christ.

This would also be stated by Herman Hoeksema: "He must have the power of faith before he can believe, the gift of repentance before he can repent" (Hoeksema, *Sin and Grace*, p. 73).

So, if man needs to receive faith from God before he can believe on Jesus, how are we to understand the following? "In those days came John the Baptist, preaching in the wilderness of Judaea, And saying, Repent, ye: for the kingdom of heaven is at hand" (Matthew 3:1-2).

And in the next chapter, the Lord Jesus Himself would echo John the Baptist: "From that time Jesus began to preach, and to say, Repent: for the kingdom of heaven is at hand" (Matthew 4:17).

So, man is clearly able to repent, without God needing to help him. And please remember that John spent six years preaching in the wilderness, and Matthew tells us how all of believing Judea, Jerusalem, and all of the believing region round about Jordan came out to be baptized (Matthew 3:5). However, not all of these baptized people would later believe on Christ when He came!

Paul would also call on the multitudes to repent, for in Acts 11:18 the reader is told how God has already (past tense) granted repentance to the Gentiles; therefore, when Paul confronted the pagan Athenians in Acts 17:30, there is no reason for these people not to conform to God's command either. And let us not forget that in Acts 5:31 that God also granted (past tense) repentance to the Jews as well.

So, when we examine these verses together, we discover quite simply how God has already granted repentance to the Jews and the Gentiles. Now, all that He expects individuals to do is to believe on Jesus when presented with the gospel.

Who can come to the Father?

Jesus said God would draw all men to Him in order to save them from their sins (John 6:44). When we use Scripture with Scripture (1 Corinthians 2:13), we discover in John 12:32, that if He, [Jesus] be lifted up from the earth (which He was when He ascended into Heaven) that He would draw all men to Himself. And in John 16:8, the Holy Ghost fulfils this Trinitarian commission by reproving the whole world of sin.

We also read from John 1:9: "*That* was the true Light, which lighteth every man that cometh into the world."

So, not only do the elect have the Light of Christ once they have appropriated the atonement, but so does every living soul since creation. However, this Light is not sufficient for one to be saved in itself. A person must believe and receive Christ for salvation for it to be sufficient.

Grace or faith, which is the gift?

"For by grace are ye saved through faith; and that not of yourself: *it is* the gift of God" (Ephesians 2:8).

All Calvinists believe that faith, as well as grace, are gifts given from God for those that will believe, i.e., the elect. In his *Study Bible*, John MacArthur says the following regarding this verse: "Although men are required to believe for salvation [how can a dead man believe on God?], even that faith is part of the gift of God which saves and cannot be exercised by one's own power" (MacArthur, *The MacArthur Study Bible*, p. 1805).

R.C. Sproul also echoes MacArthur: "The faith by which we are saved it is a gift....it is given to us" (Sproul, p. 119).

Yet, if one turns to Romans 5:15-18, it will be seen that the Holy Spirit has defined what this gift is: "But not as the offence, so also *is* the free gift. For if through the offence of one many be dead, much more the grace of God, and the gift by grace, *which is* by one man, Jesus Christ, hath abounded unto many. And not as *it was* by one that sinned, *so is* the gift: for the judgment was by one to condemnation, but the free gift *is* of many offences unto justification. For if by one man's offence death reigned by one; much more they which receive abundance of grace and of the gift of righteousness shall reign in life by one, Jesus Christ. Therefore as by the offence of one *judgment came* upon all men to condemnation; even so by the righteousness of one *the free gift came* upon all men unto justification of life."

"For the wages of sin *is* death; but the gift of God *is* eternal life through Jesus Christ our Lord" (Romans 6:23). So, using Scripture with Scripture, we see very clearly that grace is the gift of God, not faith.

Another verse that is used by Calvinists would be Romans 9:15: "I will have mercy on whom I will have mercy, and I will have compassion on whom I will have compassion." Once again, if we use Scripture to interpret Scripture, this verse is defined in the same epistle just two chapters later: "For God hath concluded them all in unbelief, that he might have mercy upon all" (Romans 11:32).

We should be grateful that the Independent Fundamental Churches of America (IFCA) doctrinal statement understood this to be so: "We believe that salvation is the gift of God brought to man and received by personal faith in the Lord Jesus Christ. Salvation is the gift; faith is the hand of the heart that reaches out and receives the gift which God offers. We need to be careful not to confuse the gift with the reception of the gift."

And one other surprise would be Calvin himself: "But they commonly misinterpret this text, and restrict the word 'gift' to faith alone. But Paul is only repeating his earlier statement in other words. He does not mean that faith is the gift of God, but that salvation is given to us by God, or, that we obtain it by the gift of God" (Calvin, *Commentaries*, Vol. II, p. 145).

One other verse that should be mentioned would be Titus 2:11: "For the grace of God that bringeth salvation hath appeared to all men."

What about the Great Commission?

Calvinist Kevin Fralick states: "The population of heaven after the end of the world will not be determined by those who have accepted the Lord Jesus Christ, but by those whom the Lord Jesus Christ accepted before the beginning."

"If Election guarantees the salvation of all that are predestinated to be saved, why should we bother with evangelism, personal or missionary? What possible difference can it make whether we speak to men or not"? (Custance, p. 277).

"God has an elect people and Christ died for them and they all will be born again and will live in heaven; all due to his sovereign grace. Many of them will have never heard the gospel" (Garrett, *Two Salvations*, p. 3).

The latter quote should cause all Bible-believing Christians to feel very concerned and horrified by what Garrett said. Not only is this totally unscriptural, but I believe it makes grace very cheap! Something non-Calvinists are often charged with!

Ruckman offers the following thoughts to this kind of deranged thinking: "Twentieth century Calvinists are totally defunct in all branches of soul winning and evangelism. They live off the glory of a handful of Calvinists back in the eighteenth and nineteenth centuries. They do not like to be reminded that although Spurgeon was a great Baptist preacher, he won less than half the number of sinners to Jesus Christ than Billy Sunday did, less than one quarter as many as Dwight L.

Moody did, and less than one-eighth as many as John Wesley did" (Ruckman, p. 47).

Yet Garrett is in very good company, for even Billy Graham and the late John Paul II both said the same thing. Graham believed there are heathen throughout the world who have never heard of Jesus, yet God will accept their pagan worship as a "substitute" for His true gospel. The late pope would also say that all those who lead a "good life" would get to Heaven. So, on this view alone, hyper-Calvinists and Catholics are in total agreement as to how it will all work out in the end!

Just when we thought we were back on more solid ground, another Calvinist comes along, with the following to offer: "For us to say that one must hear the gospel in order to be saved for heaven, it would severely limit the Holy One of Israel." (Ellis, *The Christian Baptist*, April 1993, p. 3).

Any Bible-believing student of the word of God knows that the above is totally nonsensical. Mankind has to hear the gospel in order to be saved (Mark 16:15-16).

For if he doesn't hear the gospel, how then is he expected to be saved (Romans 10:14-17)?

It doesn't take long, however, for more moderate Calvinists to regain control of their system and come back into line with a more moderate and Biblical understanding of Scripture. The ecumenical Anglican Calvinist, J.I. Packer said: "That God in the gospel really does offer Christ and promise justification and life to whosoever will" (Packer, *Evangelism and the Sovereignty of God*, p. 100).

Yet Packer doesn't really believe this. I mean how could he? According to him, Christ died for only the elect. Again this is inconstant and double talk aimed at appeasing his non-Calvinist/ecumenical friends in the apostate churches' together movement.

And not only does Packer present us with such double talk, so too does Sproul: "The Calvinist view of predestination teaches that God actively intervenes in the lives of the elect to make absolutely sure that they are saved. Of course the rest are invited to Christ and given an 'opportunity' to be saved if they want to" (Sproul, p. 34).

Well, the latter part of that paragraph is all very well, but if "others" do come, there's no blood for them, for He only died for the elect. Confused? So am I!

As has already been stated, the Wesley brothers were very much in the front line when it came to repealing the pagan philosophies of Calvinism in their day. One of John Wesley's most damning statements against the disastrous TULIP would have to be the following: "[Calvinism] represents our Lord as a hypocrite, a deceiver of the people, a man void of common sincerity, as mocking his helpless creatures by offering what he never intends to give, by saying one thing and meaning another" (Schaff, Vol. 8, p. 566).

And let us not forget the "infamous" and "loathed" Jacob Arminius: "I am fully persuaded, that the doctrine of Irresistible Grace is repugnant to the Sacred Scriptures, to all the Ancients, and to our own Confession and Catechism"

(Arminius, Vol. 1, p. 301-302).

I would say that with quotes from certain Calvinists from above, is it any wonder there are so many "lazy" and "absent" Christians on the streets! And yet false religions seem to be out in abundance, peddling their worthless and powerless "gospels."

Perseverance of the Saints

Spurgeon once said: "I do not believe in the perseverance of the saints. I believe in the perseverance of the Saviour" (Hutson, p. 17).

I thought that the last section of the TULIP system would be the easiest to write about, but it has in fact been the most challenging.

For while I hold to the eternal security of all genuine and regenerated sinners, I know that some will take exception to this. I once tried to explain to two Mormon missionaries who were knocking on doors in my town that once a person has believed on Jesus as their Lord and Saviour, he or she is saved and sealed forever (Ephesians 4:30). The missionaries then asked me: "What would happen to a Christian if they murdered a person? Surely they would lose their salvation, wouldn't they?" "No," I replied. "If a person is saved, they are still saved." A person, after being justified by faith in Christ alone, cannot be unjustified, any more than a person who is literally born cannot be literally unborn. Samson and David had people murdered/killed after they had been saved; yet they are in Heaven today.

(Incidentally, the reason this question was asked by the Mormons is because they believe some sins are so bad - murder being one - that a blood atonement from a third party may be needed if the "faithful" Mormon ever hopes to one day become a god).

To his credit, MacArthur understands how eternal security works perfectly well: "No sin a believer can commit – past, present, or future – can be held against him, since that penalty was paid by Christ and His righteousness was imputed to the believer. No sin will ever reverse this divine legal decision" (MacArthur, *Study Bible*, p. 1706).

No doubt there will be some self-righteous Christians reading this who will be fuming with me on this point, so let's take a more detailed look at some of the saved saints in the Bible, and see how they lived while in the flesh, awaiting the transformation of their vile bodies (Philippians 3:21).

King David was saved and anointed with the Holy Ghost when only a youth (1 Samuel 16:13), yet he would go on to break six of the Ten Commandments, with two of them demanding the death penalty:

– lying, deception, treason (1 Samuel 27-30)

– adultery (Deuteronomy 22:22)

– got a man drunk and then had this man killed (Exodus 21:12-14, 22-23)

Yet David was saved during this whole period, for if it had been possible for him to have lost his salvation, he would have (Hebrews 10:26).

Only after the prophet Nathan confronted him, did David finally repent. And although he begged God not to take the Holy Spirit from him, there is no reason to come to the conclusion this was meant for his salvation. He was speaking of his priestly anointing, which only Old Testament saints enjoyed.

The very night he saw Bathsheba, he slept with her (2 Samuel 11:4).

Due to his carnal desire for her, and later him learning that she had fallen pregnant by him, he allowed the enemies of Israel to kill her husband, a faithful son of Israel (2 Samuel 12:14). Consequently, God in His infinite mercy did not have David executed but spared him (2 Samuel 12:13), although due to David and Bathsheba's adultery, their firstborn child died (2 Samuel 12:15-18).

Yet David has full assurance that in the resurrection, he will see his child again. And the Lord appears to bless polygamous David, for he would have intercourse again with Bathsheba and subsequently, not only would Solomon be born but two other sons as well (2 Samuel 12:24; 1 Chronicles 3:5).

As God is no respecter of persons and as Solomon was an infamous idolater, one could speculate that infants that die young or prematurely are not Hell bound but Heaven bound).

And for Christians that fear that they might lose the Holy Spirit, they would do well to remember that the Father and the Son also reside in them, but nobody ever talks about losing the first and second members of the Godhead.

Although God heard David's beautiful prayer of repentance (Psalm 51), he still suffered terribly for his sins. For according to the Law, David should have been put to death with his mistress, but God chose His own punishment for David instead.

Four acts of retribution would follow: 1) David and Bathsheba's baby died. 2) Amnon, one of David's sons, raped his half-sister. David refused to punish this act, so for two long years, bitterness and anger built up within David's family and servants. 3) Absalom, furious that his father failed to deal with this, hatched a plot to kill his half-brother for revenge for his sister's rape. Again, David failed to respond to this act of murder with righteous judgment. 4) David did not punish him, even though he knew all along where he was hiding (2 Samuel 14:21).

And this family tragedy, in which several crimes were committed (three of which demand capital punishment), would go from bad to worse, for Absalom tried to take his father's throne from him, and at one stage consented to his father's murder (2 Samuel 17:4). All during this tragic turmoil 20,000 men perished (2 Samuel 18:7).

In the end, the coup was thwarted and David would go on to lose another son when Joab killed Absalom while he was trapped, hanging from a tree. This devastating news was too much for David, for he had told Joab and others to spare this renegade's life, even after he had had intercourse with David's concubines. The text doesn't tell us whether this act was consensual or not. With so many fatalities, David grieved for his son's death, even though the kingdom was almost destroyed; yet his attention was towards his disloyal and wicked son.

In 2 Samuel, David's transgression, in numbering all of Israel with a census, would cause the death of some 70,000 people; due to a pestilence that God had sent them (2 Samuel 24:15).

This great king was saved when only a youth, died at a good old age, full of days, riches and honour (1 Chronicles 29:28), yet his sins nearly destroyed him and his kingdom. The results of such sins would last his lifetime and beyond.

David even acknowledged that all the evil which came upon him was from God as punishment (2 Samuel 16:10).

So, if a Christian is going to lead a carnal life, be warned! Everything you cherish and all those that you love will suffer! You might lose your job, house, friends, family, money, health, and possibly even die, but if you are saved, then you will remain forever saved!

King Solomon: David affirms that God chose Solomon to be king (1 Chronicles 28:5). David also makes it clear that blessings will come to Solomon if he obeys God, and curses will come if he disobeys God. However, Deuteronomy 31:16-21 states that future disobedience would plague Israel – Solomon's sins resulted in his breaking several commandments, with two calling for the death penalty, i.e., idolatry and adultery. God warned Solomon about the consequences of disobedience (2 Chronicles 7:17-22), yet this king was not only chosen by God (before the foundation of the world according to Calvinists), twice communed with God; led a great multitude of people; had kings and queens from all over the world come to seek his wisdom; built the temple for the Lord - something David wasn't allowed to do -, a whole chapter in 2 Chronicles 6 is given to his prayer, with Solomon on his knees throughout, yet I believe he remained saved all along.

And does not 2 Samuel 7:14-15 tell us how God would not take His mercy from Solomon as He did with Saul?

This passage promises: "I will be his father, and he shall be my son. If he commit iniquity, I will chasten him with the rod of men, and with the stripes of the children of men: But my mercy shall not depart away from him, as I took *it* from Saul, whom I put away before thee."

Solomon was saved when he was old enough to comprehend God, something that is still applicable today for Christian youths.

The writer below, under the inspiration of the Holy Ghost, offers the following about this wayward king: "Did not Solomon king of Israel sin by these things? Yet among many nations was there no king like him, who was beloved of his God, and God made him king over Israel: nevertheless even him did outlandish women cause to sin" (Nehemiah 13:26).

King Saul: "Because thou obeyedst not the voice of the LORD, nor executedst his fierce wrath upon Amalek, therefore hath the LORD done this thing unto thee this day. Moreover the LORD will also deliver Israel with thee into the hand of the Philistines: and to morrow *shalt* thou and thy sons *be* with me: the LORD also shall deliver the host of Israel into the hand of the Philistines" (1 Samuel 28:18-19).

Based on the premise that Samuel was saved (Hebrews 11:32), and based on the premise from Luke 16:19-31 that Hell (known also in the Bible as the pit, Gehenna, Hades, etc.) is in the ground, and based on the premise that everyone, saved or unsaved, all went into the ground upon death, pre-Christ, we can ascertain from this piece of Scripture alone that Samuel, upon death, was in the ground, along with Saul's sons, awaiting Saul to join them all within 24 hours.

Also, we know from the first death (Luke 16:19-31) how the righteous dead were unable to cross over and interact with the unrighteous dead. All they were permitted to do was speak to one another from their relevant sections.

So, Samuel's words to Saul about 'to morrow *shalt* thou and thy sons *be* with me' must be taken literally. Saul would soon be with Samuel and his sons in the righteous part of hell, albeit arriving with nothing to show for his life. (This pictures a carnal Christian arriving at the Judgment Seat of Christ, saved, but still with nothing to show for their Christian life).

Lot was called just and righteous (2 Peter 2:7-8), yet he was prepared to offer up his virgin daughters to a crowd of sodomites. He lost his wife, and his daughters lost their virginities, but he was saved (1 Corinthians 3:15).

Jacob lied about his birthright, deceived his father twice, pretending to be his brother Esau, and even told him how God gave him his food, which Isaac had sent Esau out for (Genesis 27:20). When Esau came for him, he aligned his family into positions so as to avoid those he loved the most being hurt

(Genesis 33:2), yet he was saved (Hebrews 11:21).

Samson was a fornicator, murdered thirty men for their garments, committed suicide and murdered many Philistines as well, yet he was saved throughout (Hebrews 11:32-35).

So, while the Bible says we can live above sin when we walk in the Spirit, we can't live permanently without sin in our lives: "If we say that we have not sinned, we make him a liar, and his word is not in us" (1 John 1:10).

This verse is also something that every Old Testament saint adhered to (1 Kings 8:46).

We must remember, of course, that the Old Testament was written so that Christians wouldn't make the same mistakes (1 Corinthians 10:11). However, there is no reason to conclude that people today can't be as sinful or even worse than their forefathers were (vs. 12).

I remember once discussing with a pastor whether or not I had to "continue in the faith" if I hoped to ever be saved. I responded by saying: "If my salvation depends on me continuing to do a, b and c, then I would lose my salvation tomorrow." I still believe this to be so, and I am quite content to tell people I meet that one is saved (past tense) by what Jesus did for them, not by what one does for Him. In other words, His substitutionary death and one's faith in it is all that Scripture teaches is needed to be saved. Once saved, then works would naturally follow.

Yet, if saved people have to persevere in order to be saved, what would happen if they didn't persevere enough? Or if they did persevere, then they are not saved by faith alone (something all Calvinists hold to) but by faith and works, something Catholics would certainly agree with. And if faith and works were needed, then every Catholic that I knew would be saved?! And how would a person know if they had endured enough? Or if they hadn't endured enough, would it be possible for them to know before death? Would they lose their salvation for not "enduring" enough? Or would they be disqualified? And if they did lose their salvation, when might they expect to be made aware of this? What sin would need to be committed for the loss of salvation (Jude 16:20)? And of course, according to Hebrews 10:26, if you could lose it, you'd never get it back!

So, I have to ask the same question again: either one is saved or not. Holy and godly living are one thing, and they are certainly elements that should be evident in each Christian's life. But if one trusts in their goodness and their religious output (Acts 17:22-23), then this too is no guarantee that one is saved. Or if one does live the "complete and supreme" Christian life, then who saved whom? Did Jesus save that person, or did that person saved himself?

Isn't this what Paul warns against in Romans 4:2: "For if Abraham were justified by works, he hath *whereof* to glory, but not before God."

The terrible consequences of lordship salvation

"Friend, if Jesus Christ isn't Lord of your life, then you are yet lost in your sins" (Otis, *Who is the Genuine Christian?*, p. 7).

"No man can accept Jesus as Saviour of his soul without accepting Him as Lord of his life" (Shank, *Life in the Son*, p. 15).

"Christians will never be ashamed at the judgment seat of Christ" (MacArthur, *Marks of a True Believer*, p. 34, 37).

According to the above Calvinists, Sproul better watch out then, for he openly acknowledges how he's addicted to ice cream, and that he doesn't totally love Christ to perfection (Sproul, pp. 56; 170).

And what about the Corinthians? Didn't some of them die due to their carnality? I'm sure many of them will be ashamed and disgusted with themselves at the Bema Seat.

A controversial teaching made news in the evangelical world in the 1990s, as the question was asked: "To be saved, does one need to believe on the Lord Jesus and make Him Lord of one's life, or can they just accept Him as Saviour"?

John Macarthur and James White declare that Jesus needs to be one's Lord and Saviour, if they are to be saved and stay saved.

Yet the late Dr. J. Vernon McGee, when asked by one of his radio listeners whether Jesus was Lord of his life said: "I accepted Christ as my Saviour. He's not Lord of my life. If that's heresy, so be it."

However, David Hocking (one of McGee's biggest admirers and one who believes in Lordship salvation) told me in an e-mail how he didn't agree with McGee on this issue. Interesting isn't it!?

So, once again, all different views from different Bible teachers, on this particular issue on Lordship salvation.

When I was a Catholic, there used to be a joke that went like this: "Pick your favourite priest for confession." Some priests would give you a lenient penance, others much harsher. The same can be said today. Pick your favourite preacher, for the view you want to have and promote.

All genuine Christians know, however, that Jesus Christ is the most important and central Figure in their lives. They love Him, live for Him and strive for Him. But to say He has to be Lord of one's life in order to then be saved and stay saved is problematic.

For example, how does one know if they've done enough to make Him Lord of their life? What happens if they slip every now and then, and then die?

According to some conditional security proponents, such a person would need to be born again, again. Yet these same people refuse to be held accountable for such a banal view. Such holiness groups will tell their congregations that if they are perfect all of the time and don't sin, then they'll be okay, but if they don't behave themselves, they might perish. Here's the problem: in Hebrews, we are told: "If we sin willfully after that we have received the knowledge of the truth, there remaineth no more sacrifice for sins" (Hebrews 10:26).

Therefore, according to conditional security proponents and all other holiness groups, this is speaking of all sins in general. Yet if they wish to use this verse and apply it doctrinally to Christians, then they have one big problem: these people are damned and can never be reconciled back to God again, even if they wanted to! So, realizing this, the conditional security proponents look elsewhere for a verse they can use to teach reconciliation to God, while at the same time, holding to one losing their salvation!

The late Barry Smith was devastated when one of his daughters committed suicide. For years this Pentecostal preacher rigorously towed his denomination's party line when it came to their belief of saved people losing their salvation. He would often tell his audience that it was blasphemy to commit suicide and may in fact be one of the unpardonable sins. Of course, Barry was wrong and only when his daughter took her own life, was he forced to leave the mainstream Pentecostal world, due primarily to their insistence that his daughter had committed blasphemy, lost her salvation, and subsequently was now in Hell. This naturally forced his re-think of this nonsensical doctrine of Christians losing their salvation, no matter what they did once saved.

And how intriguing it is when leaders such as Jimmy Swaggart and Jim Bakker both hold that you can lose your salvation if/when you sin willfully, yet neither of these men lost their salvation when they sinned! Both are still preaching today!

It may be of interest to the reader that many Calvinists don't believe in carnal Christians, or the two natures of the believer.

MacArthur states that the old nature and new nature terminology is not a Biblical term. He seems to lean to almost full sanctification, something Wesley and all holiness groups adhere to.

Yet did not MacArthur recently buy the copyright to all his books? This would have cost him a small fortune, and was no doubt done to secure his financial interests as a worldwide writer. What's wrong with this, some might ask? Nothing, but I wasn't the person who said that "he would be happy to eat grass," or that "money meant nothing to him." MacArthur said this, not me.

The late Harry Ironside said the following about the two natures: "The flesh in the believer is no better than the flesh in an unbeliever."

There are however, several Calvinists who take issue with MacArthur's views on Lordship salvation: "MacArthur attacks justification by faith alone and suggests that works be understood as part of faith" (Robbins, *The Gospel According to John MacArthur*, part 1, p. 1).

"MacArthur's book [*The Gospel According to Jesus*] is very confused and dangerous. It does not present the Gospel according to Jesus, but another gospel, which is not a gospel at all, similar to that of the Roman Church" (John Robbins, *The Gospel According to John MacArthur*, part 2; p. 2).

This last statement is devastating to MacArthur, for not only is he accused of preaching a false gospel, but is also dubbed a semi-Arminian. However, on this subject Pink correctly held to the Biblical teaching concerning carnality and the twin natures in all Christians (Vance, pp. 580-581).

However Pink and Garrett both hold to these Biblical facts, concerning carnality and the twin natures, in all Christians (2 p. 580-581).

Must the elect persevere till the end to be saved?

"And ye shall be hated of all men for my name's sake: but he that endureth to the end shall be saved" (Matthew 10:22).

"But he that shall endure unto the end, the same shall be saved" (Matthew 24:13).

Here are two totally opposite views on these most controversial verses.

First, from a reformed Calvinist, who was one of the editors for the *New International Bible Commentary*, 1997, based on the NIV: "To follow Jesus is not a route to popularity and influence; it leads to life on the run (vs. 23a). But vs. 23b assures the Twelve that their mission would not be complete before the Son of Man comes. However often they were repulsed, there would always be more of the cities of Israel to take the message to" (Bruce, *New International Bible Commentary*, p. 917).

In contrast, a fundamentalist Baptist has said, "The end has no reference to the end of their lives, and it is aimed at 'them,' referring to the people to whom they are getting ready to witness... no way refers to the destruction of Jerusalem in A.D. 70, for many who endured to this end were not saved. Furthermore, many who were saved spiritually were killed physically before, during, and after 'the end'... to make matters worse, many of the 'saved' did not endure to the end of A.D. 70 and died before A.D. 50 (1 Corinthians 15:5-10)" (Ruckman,

Certainly Paul finished his course, kept his faith, and won his crown that the Lord had set him (2 Timothy 4:7). But is this something that is applicable to all believers? Didn't the Lord tell Paul that he would have to take the gospel to kings and leaders, and suffer many things for Him (Acts 9:15)? So wouldn't it be fair to say that Paul was somewhat of a special case? However, the apostle did say that the crown that awaited him would also be for others too. Yet what crown are we referring to? I believe this crown is one of five that Scripture speaks of: the crown of life (or martyr's crown), the crown of glory (this is an elder's or pastor's crown), the crown of rejoicing (the "soul winner's crown," i.e., those brought to Jesus by us), the crown of righteousness (the crown for those who love His appearing, given in that day) and the incorruptible crown (this is the victor's crown to the one who did not yield, nor was diverted from the work of the Master).

Friends, salvation is not the subject here. What is being discussed are rewards for those that are already saved. This is what Paul was enduring for, not his own salvation.

As God's elect nation, Israel was the smallest and least important of all nations (Deuteronomy 7:7), yet they rebelled against God (2 Kings 17:20-21), and at one stage a pagan Gentile king sent for one of their priests to teach them the way of God (2 Kings 17:27-28): they were worse than the pagan nations at times (2 Kings 21:9; 2 Chronicles 33:9). Not only did they not all persevere with Him, they weren't even faithful to Him, yet because God strived with them, and because God kept His oath, which he had sworn with their fathers (Deuteronomy 7:8), they were never cast away. Yes, many would die physically, but there is no need to believe they perished forever.

In Isaiah 65:2-5, we read: "I have spread out my hands all the day unto a rebellious people, which walketh in a way *that was* not good, after their own thoughts; A people that provoketh me to anger continually to my face; that sacrificeth in gardens, and burneth incense upon altars of brick; Which remain among the graves, and lodge in the monuments, which eat swine's flesh, and broth of abominable *things is in* their vessels; Which say, Stand by thyself, come not near to me; for I am holier than thou. These *are* a smoke in my nose, a fire that burneth all the day."

Moses disobeyed God (Numbers 20:12) and was still full of life when he was put to death prematurely by God, yet he was saved (Hebrews 11:23-29).

Moses disobeyed God (Num. 20:12), was still full of life when he was put to death prematurely by God, yet he was saved (Heb. 11:23-29).

Aaron broke the 2nd Commandment (something punishable by death,

Deuteronomy 27:15), and failed to confess this fully when confronted by Moses (Exodus 32:22-24), and therefore along with Moses, died prematurely, yet there is no reason to doubt he wasn't saved.

In New Testament theology, the following Calvinists line up, with their take on this: "The doctrine declares that once God has begun the work of salvation in any person, He will preserve therein to the end and will never let any of His own be lost" (Rose, *T.U.L.I.P.: The Five Disputed Points of Calvinism*, p. 49).

MacArthur would certainly not agree with this statement, for he believes that one needs to live righteously and persevere, if one is to be saved: "The ones who persevere are the same ones who are saved – not the ones whose love grows cold" (MacArthur, *Study Bible*, p. 1439).

Yet before long, another Calvinist is found who agrees with MacArthur too: "This doctrine teaches that those who truly have come to saving faith in Christ will preserve in the faith" (*Grover Gunn*, p. 24).

"Perseverance is what we do. Preservation is what God does. We persevere because God preserves" (Sproul, p. 175).

All this may sound good, but my question is this: How does one know if they are persevering enough? How can one know for sure if their level of holiness is sufficient to demonstrate that they really are saved? And what would happen to such a person if they committed a sin, never confessed it, and then died?

According to Pink and other Calvinists like him: "Those who persevere not in faith and holiness, love and obedience, will assuredly perish" (Pink, *Eternal Security*, p. 28). And yet as no Christian has ever lived to perfection, how can they know if they've made the mark?

Even Hebrews 12:4 declares this: "Ye have not yet resisted unto blood, striving against sin."

Calvinists correctly inform their audience that when Paul tells us how we've missed the mark, and that even when we're saved, we still continue to totally miss it, how can these views hold up? (Romans 3:23). Either one is totally justified by the finished work of Christ or not! Once a person is saved, is he expected to work to stay saved? Surely if a sinner cannot save himself before he's saved (Romans 4:4), then he certainly cannot help himself after he's saved!?

Some seem to think that when sinners become saints, they become partners with God, at least a very junior partner, in the process of "bringing about glorification." So, I ask this simple question: Either a person is saved when he/she believes on the Lord, or not. Which is it?

Billy Sunday once said that Christians will fall in the mud (the world's system), roll around in it for a while (enjoy the sin), but eventually get up, repent of this and continue on in the faith, until the next time they stumble. The unsaved man, however, like all dogs and unclean animals, loves the mud, desires to always be rolling around in this filth, has no intention of ever doing anything else, for it is all he knows.

Calvinist Steven Houck finds a similar analogy: "Though the true believer may slip into grievous sin, he does not fall absolutely. God brings him back so that by faith he walks in the ways of God. He is preserved in the way of faith – a faith that results in godly living" (Houck, *God's Sovereignty in Salvation,*

p. 32).

Or another helpful expression: "A believer may fall inboard but never overboard."

Now of course, not all people agree with these statements. Please see what John Otis said on this: "Falling away from the Faith, doesn't mean that one loses his salvation, it means that one never had any salvation from the beginning" (Otis, *Who is the Genuine Christian?*, p. 40).

I return to my early point: What about the carnal Corinthians then? Were they all unsaved? Paul never said they were, only that many of them slept, a meaning they were dead in the Lord, not dead and lost in Hell.

Lawrence Vance stated, "Calvinists emphasise continuance in believing and living in holiness to the end of one's life much like the Arminian would do" (Vance, p. 559).

So, is the old sound bite, "once saved, always saved" considered orthodox theology or not?

Please see what the following leading Calvinists say: "[This doctrine] of once saved, always saved is one of the grandest of Biblical teachings" (Palmer, p. 79).

Yet, if one holds to the second and third aspect of TULIP, then surely they would expect this to be so, for surely God would never allow one of His elected saints to perish, if He chose them in eternity past?

Anthony Hoekema: "The Canons of Dort do not in any way

support the erroneous understanding of this doctrine that some seem to have, namely, 'Once saved, always saved', regardless of how we live" (Hoekema, *Saved by Grace*, p. 253-254).

So, if one lives correctly, then they are saved? But if one doesn't, then they're damned? How can this be? Again, either a person has passed from death to life (John 5:24) or he hasn't. How can a saved sinner, covered in His Saviour's imputed righteousness, add anything further to his perfect salvation? Of course a saint can live carnally, which all do from time to time, but nothing and nobody can keep a justified and sanctified saint from Heaven (Rom. 8:38). Yet according to Calvinists, Jesus may refuse them entry to the Kingdom, if they haven't been perfect, after being saved!

On page xx, *The MacArthur Study Bible* lists the following points to look out for, when checking one's spiritual life:

Are you saved by faith in Jesus Christ (1 Corinthians 2:14-16)?

Are you hungering for God's Word (1 Peter 2:2)?

Are you searching God's Word with diligence (Acts 17:11)?

Are you seeing holiness (1 Peter 1:14-16)?

Are you Spirit-filled (Colossians 3:16)?

While I can appreciate these helpful and useful pointers, I am still unsure whether one can give a resounding "yes" to the 2nd, 3rd, 4th, and 5th to absolute perfection? What if one is lagging in some of these areas? What if one goes through a dry period?

Does this mean they are not saved? I was once told how saved people "don't have dry periods."

Yet the Calvinist pastor Warren Wiersbe spoke of times when he was so dry, he couldn't preach. Others in his church had to step in for him.

I have also heard of numerous pastors needing long sabbaticals to "reconnect" with God, so I believe it's more common than some would like us to believe.

What is faith, or how much faith do I need for Heaven?

Paul told the petrified Philippian jailer, who knew he would be executed by his Roman superiors for failing to secure the prison, to simply believe on the Lord Jesus to be saved (Acts 16:30-31).

That's all!

In Romans 10:9: "That if thou shalt confess with thy mouth the Lord Jesus, and shalt believe in thine heart that God hath raised him from the dead, thou shalt be saved."

Are these verses clear or not? Does a person need to add works to be saved? Or how many "good works" does the potential Christian need to be saved and to "stay saved"?

A.W. Pink suggests that works are necessary: "There is a deadly and damnable heresy being widely propagated today to the effect that, if a sinner truly accepts Christ as his personal Saviour, no matter how he lives afterwards, he cannot perish. This is a satanic lie, for it is at direct variance with the teaching of the Word of truth. Something more than believing in Christ is necessary to ensure the soul's reaching heaven" (Murray, *The Life of Arthur W Pink*, pp. 248-249).

Maybe Pink was a closet Catholic all along. He was certainly more at home with them, as the following quote affirms from the Council of Trent: "If anyone says that a man once justified cannot lose grace and therefore that he falls and sins never was truly justified, let him be accursed" (6/23).

Rome knows that *Sola Fide* (faith alone for salvation) is deadly for her religious structure, for if she held to this correct Biblical doctrine, then her whole apparatus will collapse. If souls are saved by faith in Christ alone, then people need not go to her church or any church for that matter.

Think about it for a moment. If sinners are saved by faith in Christ alone, something all Bible believers hold to, then nobody needs to ever go to church. People would only go to church because they are saved, not because they want to be saved. Rome understands this very well, for the word "alone" has to be dropped, and curses put on those that threaten her pagan priesthood.

Did not Paul in Galatians 3:3 tell the church that faith alone was sufficient for salvation? One is saved, therefore, simply by his or her faith in Christ alone. I would have to agree with Paul, when he totally rejects the anticipated criticism from those who were going to oppose him on justification by faith alone: "What shall we say then? Shall we continue in sin, that grace may abound?

God forbid" (Romans 6:1-2a).

Or as one Bible teacher helpfully noted: "We want to live our lives to His glory and to please Him." This is very true and I would concur with it 100%. Like children who are forever trying to be like their parents and please them, Christians desperately and consistently long to honour and please the Lord. But I cannot agree with Pink on the latter part of his statement. Faith is all God wants from imperfect people, and this is all imperfect people can give Him. Otherwise, if man can live righteously enough to enter Heaven, Jesus wouldn't have needed to become a substitutionary Saviour for man in the first place.

Lewis Sperry Chafer: "This one word 'believe' represents all a sinner can do and all a sinner must do to be saved" (Chafer, *Salvation*, p. 33).

Legalism undermines true salvation

"Those who do not love their neighbour, especially those of the household of faith, are yet lost in their sins" (Otis, *Who is the Genuine Christian?*, pp. 22- 23).

"Reader, if there is a reserve in your obedience, you are on your way to hell" (Pink, *Practical Christianity*, p. 16).

If these extreme views were to be considered as serious and helpful contributions to the Body of Christ by able scholars, then one would wonder how the apostle Peter stood when the episode of Galatians 2:11-14 occurred? Certainly he showed no "reserve in his obedience" to the Gospel (Acts 15:19-29).

Or perhaps he, until that stage at least, wasn't saved? Or maybe according to the above Pharisees, he was never saved?!

The problem with legalism is it makes salvation a yoke (Acts 15:10), something Jesus said He'd come to remove (Matthew 11:30). It also takes away any joy, peace and assurance of salvation that the Christian may have, and causes him/her to become dragged down with the burden of being unable to reach perfection all of time, every time.

As nobody ever kept the law of God perfectly (John 7:19; James 2:10), then how are we, while living under grace, expected to? And if Old Testament saints couldn't do it – Calvinists believe they too were regenerated as we are – then it is certain that New Testament saints won't deal much better either.

One other danger with legalism is the false teaching that one needs to continue to live holy in order to stay saved, or to demonstrate one was initially elected in the first place to salvation.

132

Can I lose my salvation?

Charles Hodge tragically believed the apostle Paul – a man who had seen the three heavens, wrote nearly half of the New Testament, and was called brother before he was even baptized – could have lost his eternal salvation when he spoke of himself being a castaway if he didn't control his body (1 Corinthians 9:27): "This devoted apostle considered himself as engaged in a life struggle for his salvation" (Hodge, *1 Corinthians*, p. 169).

For anyone to seriously believe this is quite amazing!

Then Robert Shank makes the same blunder: "Paul's fear was the possibility of losing, not opportunities or rewards for service, but the salvation of his own soul" (Shank, *Life in the Son*, p. 37).

Please allow me to again quote Sproul, who offers a rather self-righteous thought: "We are to work hard, resisting sin unto blood if necessary, pummelling our bodies if that is what it takes to subdue them" (Sproul, p. 158).

How sad and tragic it is that such men as this really believe that one can slip out of the Lord's hand (John 10:28-30). One must also come to the conclusion that men, such as these "super-duper" Christians, must be so holy and saintly all of the time that perhaps God should have chosen them instead of Paul to be His victorious apostle; for these men would *never* have come near to losing their salvation!

A quick re-read of Hebrews 12:4 brings us back to earth with a crash.

Other passages that haunt certain believers into concluding that a bought sinner can lose his salvation would be Hebrews and 2 Peter. Both these books, however, need to be understood in their correct context.

For example, Hebrews is not only the epistle parallel to Leviticus, it's also clearly aimed at Jewish Christians not Gentile Christians. (1 Corinthians 10:32). Now please don't misunderstand me. I am not saying that this book is only for the Jews; but may I quote J Vernon McGee: "It's all for us, but it's not all to us." In other words, the Bible is for all those that believe on the Lord, but the teachings aren't applicable to everybody living in different dispensations. I would also immediately refute the slander that I might be one of those who is quite happy to carve up the word of God and take from it what I want.

The Bible is a Jewish Book, written by Jewish men, for Jewish people. The Messiah of Israel was Jewish. His apostles were all Jewish, and every writer of the New Testament was Jewish. Therefore one would do well to remember that the Jews are God's main concern and interest, and this is especially presented in the New Testament.

When Jesus died, the dividing wall of separation between Jew and Gentile was about to be brought crashing down (Ephesians 2:12-13). With both groups now being seen as one in the eyes of God (Galatians 3:28), all that was left was for the writers of Scripture to make sure that the Jews who had come to Christ would remain faithful in their faith in Christ. In other words, once they had received Him, there was no turning back to Judaism or one's good works (John 6:66; Romans 10:1-4).

If a sinner is saved, justified and being sanctified, it is thus impossible for such a person to slip into sin and go to Hell.

The Bible teaches that we are now the sons of God (1 John 3:2), bone of His bone and flesh of His flesh (Ephesians 5:3), and sealed by the Holy Ghost (Ephesians 4:30). Therefore, it is totally nonsensical, insane and probably even sinful for saints of God who have passed from death to life (John 5:24), who are being conformed to His image on a daily basis (Romans 8:29), who were promised they would never be cast out (John 6:37), to ever believe that they or others could still perish and go to Hell! Such folks should spend their time worshiping and praising their Lord and Saviour and not waste their time, or His time, worrying about a demonic doctrine of losing their salvation and subsequently being severed from His own body!

The Bible does speak, however, about endurance and the need for one to better their walk with the Saviour.

We should also be mindful that even if a faithful saint - loved and adored by the local church - fell into sin, left their church and never returned, they shouldn't be so quickly written off. There is too much of a tendency to say things like: "Oh, well, he wasn't ever saved in the first place." Or: "Well, he's lost his salvation now. God's given him up."

Such talk is certainly immature and potentially poisonous. What a local church doesn't know is that such a person might come back to the Lord later on!

I once knew a brother who fell away from the Lord for twelve years. He left his wife and kids and then during that time returned to his old life of gambling. No doubt his friends and family wrote him off, but you know what? He repented and later returned to the Lord, even attempting to win souls to Him.

The following verses are often used to argue that those that are saved can lose their salvation, if they don't continue in the faith. I don't believe this. I have come to the opinion that the following Scriptures are indeed speaking to the 1st century Jews at the time as well as to Jews in a future time period (Tribulation Jews). Of course, the entire Bible is written to us (all people) but it's not all for us (different time periods!)

"They [false Jewish disciples, teachers and prophets which went back to Judaism] went out from us [true sanctified and justified believers in Jesus], but they were not of us; for if they had been of us, they would *no doubt* have continued with us: but *they went out*, that they might be made manifest that they were not all of us" (1 John 2:19).

"And let us consider one another to provoke unto love and to good works: Not forsaking the assembling of ourselves together [being identified with other Jewish Christians in a public way], as the manner of some *is*; but exhorting *one another*: and so much the more, as ye see the day approaching" (Hebrews 10:24-25).

Interesting to read the above statement, about unity and

identity with Christ, not Judaism!

"For if we sin wilfully [Jewish people rejecting Christ, His atonement and returning to Judaism after being baptized into Him] after that we have received the knowledge of the truth [this could refer to only faith in Jesus, John 14:6], there remaineth no more sacrifice for sins, But a certain fearful looking for of judgment and fiery indignation, which shall devour the adversaries. [Christ is the only substitutionary atonement for man] He that despised Moses' law died without mercy under two or three witnesses: Of how much sorer punishment, suppose ye, shall he be thought worthy, who hath trodden under foot the Son of God, and hath counted the blood of the covenant, wherewith he was sanctified, an unholy thing, and hath done despite unto the Spirit of grace"? (Hebrews 10:26).

May I say the following concerning this passage: Some prophecy teachers believe this is speaking to Jews in the Tribulation. I have heard of Christians, and please don't ask me how, falling into cults and even the occult, yet years later, they've repented of this and returned to Christ. Nobody in their local church refused them entry, and nobody as far as I am aware doubted their faith. Yet, if the above verses could be used today, then how would these Christians stand? People would say that perhaps they weren't saved in the first place to start with. Maybe this is so, but maybe it's not. Maybe they were saved all along, yet they had never matured as saints of Christ to resist the very strong pull of such groups.

"For if after they [false Jewish believers] have escaped the pollutions of the world through the knowledge of the Lord and Saviour Jesus Christ, they are again entangled therein, and overcome, the latter end is worse with them than the beginning" (2 Peter 2:20).

These verses clearly teach that if one "turns back" permanently to Judaism, and the reader is presented with the Biblical fact that judgment awaits such. And the language seems to suggest it may be eternal judgment.

So, how this could apply to Christians today, I don't know. Christians don't have a Jewish temple to go back to, nor would a Jewish synagogue welcome such people. What I do know, however, is that the Lord promises eternal salvation to anyone who trusts Him alone. Or as Peter so brilliantly said: "Lord, to whom shall we go? thou hast the words of eternal life" (John 6:68). And isn't this the same chapter where some of His disciples walked with Him no more (vs. 66). I wonder where they went to....back to the temple, of course! And it's these kinds of people that the New Testament speaks of, not carnal Christians who fall into sin and spend years out of fellowship with God.

If a person wants to meditate on Scripture to assure oneself that they are saved, please see the following verses: "Verily, verily, I say unto you, He that heareth my word, and believeth on him that sent me, hath everlasting life, and shall not come into condemnation; but is passed from death unto life" (John 5:24).

"But we believe that through the grace of the Lord Jesus Christ we shall be saved, even as they" (Acts 15:11).

"What shall we say then that Abraham our father, as pertaining to the flesh, hath found? For if Abraham were justified by works, he hath *whereof* to glory; but not before God. For what saith the scripture? Abraham believed God, and it was counted unto him for righteousness. Now to him that worketh is the reward not reckoned of grace, but of debt. But to him that worketh not, but believeth on him that justifieth the ungodly, his faith is counted for righteousness. Even as David also describeth the blessedness of the man, unto whom God imputeth righteousness without works, *Saying*, Blessed *are* they whose iniquities are forgiven, and whose sins are covered. Blessed *is* the man to whom the Lord will not impute sin" (Romans 4:1-7).

One other thing that I would like to demonstrate is how amazingly faithful and merciful God is.

For example, a believer is told to confess his Saviour before men (Matthew 10:32-32), but if he is unfaithful in doing this (Matthew 26:73) God cannot deny Himself, for though we may be unfaithful, He always remains faithful (2 Timothy 2:13).

Once again, Vance makes good sense when he states that Calvinists get so upset about Christians who do not persevere because of "pride and envy" (Vance, p. 577).

Yet even these "supreme" Calvinists had better be cautious, for Pink tells his reader: "To be a staunch and sound Calvinist is no evidence one is regenerate" (Vance, p. 594-595.)

Self-righteousness and pride is the cause of legalism. If one gets control over drinking and smoking, and another believer cannot, the self-righteous believer makes the sweeping declaration to his friends that this failed Christian is, in fact, still dead in his sins. Salvation has yet to come to this person. Yet what can be worse than self-righteousness? Hypocrisy, something all saints are guilty of. However, when a leading five-point Calvinist who expects perfection from others is reported to drink and smoke too, well, this person loses all credibility in the eyes of his so-called *perfect* circle of Christians (Hoeksema, *Therefore Have I Spoken*, p. 240).

And did not this same tobacco-loving Calvinist say the following about the heart of the Bible: "John 3:16 is probably the most frequently misinterpreted and misused verse in all Holy Scripture. I refer to the fact, of course, that so often it is explained as meaning that God loves all men. Nothing could be further from the truth!"

Well, Mr. Hoeksema, how should Psalm 119:160 be interpreted: "Thy word *is* true"?!?

Arminius' statement should be read and re-read by all his critics, for what he says here not only clarifies his views on one's eternal security in Christ, but very much echoes what honest and moderate Calvinists also believe: "Though I here openly and ingenuously affirm, I never taught that a true believer can either totally or finally fall away for the faith, and perish; yet I will not conceal, that there are passages of Scripture which seem to wear this aspect; and those answers to them which I have been permitted to see, are not of such a kind as to approve themselves on all points to my understanding" (Arminius, pp.

664-667).

As I've already stated, I'm convinced that Arminius must be one of the most misunderstood and despised Christians that ever lived. And why is he hated? Because Calvinists loathe the idea that they might be wrong and others correct. However, this cannot justify the character assassination that he has had to undergo, nor is it fair for non-Calvinists to be ridiculed with derogatory terms that all those that reject TULIP are really just Catholics, Jesuits or inferior Christians in the Body of Christ. The Lord Jesus at His Judgment Seat will judge such people who slander His Saints, if they themselves are even saved (Matthew 7:21-23).

Conclusion

When I started researching and compiling this manuscript in 2004, I was amazed at where most of the criticism of Calvin and his theological system comes from. One would imagine that ardent Arminians and Catholics would be the most vocal, but they're not. The most critical voices of this reformer and his views are fellow Calvinists. Philip Schaff, for example, not only held to the TULIP but was also head of the ASV committee and spoke of Calvin, in my opinion, with utter contempt.

It also appears that certain Calvinists not only blame God for every abortion, rape, murder, and other evils and wickedness, but they also seem to have no assurance of salvation themselves, nor can they know for sure if they are even one of the elect. The best they can hope for is that they live perfectly (which of course nobody does), and trust that this endurance and perseverance will be sufficient to demonstrate to themselves that they are indeed one of the elect. There are so many problems with this, I scarcely know where to begin.

For don't "good" Catholics, Mormons, and Jehovah's Witnesses endure? The ones I know do: church every day; attend all services; on multiple committees; give generously to charities and so on. So, if endurance and holiness are needed to be sure that they are the elect, then certain Catholics, in my opinion, "win" hands down. And what if a person, after believing in Christ for 50 years, starts to fall into old sins and even new ones, just before he/she dies, and never repents? Is their holiness good enough, or not? Did they really repent and believe on Jesus enough all those years ago? Do they now need to be born again, again?

Once again, Vance says it all: "The only difference between a Calvinist and an Arminian when it comes to assurance is that the Arminian requires holiness to prove salvation while the Calvinist demands holiness to demonstrate election, which then substantiates salvation" (Vance, p. 596).

May I also share with the reader this sad and ridiculous quote from the Calvinist Lorraine Boettner: "We can never know that we are elected of God to eternal life except by manifesting in our lives the fruits of election – faith and virtue, knowledge and temperance, patience and godliness, love of the brethren. It is idle to see assurance of election outside of holiness of life" (Boettner, *Predestination*, p. 309).

Some years ago I had the "good pleasure" of meeting a fanatical five-point Calvinist in Wigan town centre whenever we went there to preach and evangelise. He occasionally "proselytised" along with his friend. Each time we met, we'd lock horns. I would put my point to him, why I felt Calvin was wrong in this and that, and especially for the sixty people that were killed in Geneva. And he would fire back at me with his defence of Calvin, and on and on it would go! Then one day, I said to him: "Do you think Calvin would defend you so rigorously? I've known Catholics that would die for their pope and in the process knock down anyone to the ground that didn't agree with them and their church, so maybe you're not much different than they are? Why not fight for Jesus?" "He replied by saying to me: "Do you mean to say that Spurgeon and

Whitefield were all wrong when they said how much they had been indebted to Calvin?" I replied: "Well, these men, who still retained their old natures, turned a blind eye to Calvin's police state ("thought police").

The fact is for those that are in organised religion, they cannot really speak out against those that have gone before them. This is the difference between Biblical Christianity and organised religion. Only when one leaves organised religion, can one see its sheer folly and nonsense.

Friends, if you're in a man-made theological system (a term even coined by Calvinist W.J. Seaton on the TULIP), please get out of it!

You cannot defend men like Calvin anymore then you would Josemaría Escrivá (infamous as the founder of the Roman Catholic hyper-traditionalist organization known as Opus Dei). They will always let you down sooner or later, but Jesus Christ will never let you down. Stand for Him and on His foundation alone!

Billton echoes this: "Those who are 'Ambassadors for Calvinism' defend and put forward Calvin's ideas and doctrines and some have the arrogance to claim this as the gospel message, which in fact contradicts and dishonours Christ and His Gospel. They are far more zealous to win Christians over to Calvinism than they are to win the lost to Christ and His Kingdom! They show this in the vast amount of man hours and finance used in promoting and defending Calvinism" (Billton, p. 11).

I agree with this 100%!

So, the last word in this book goes to Curtis Hutson: "Calvinism is a philosophy developed by man and depending on fallible logic and frail, human reasoning, with the perversion of some Scriptures, the misuse of others, and the total ignorance of many clear Scriptures" (Hutson, p. 19).

Sources

Rev. C.H. Irwin, John Calvin, The man and his work, 1909 (Calvinist)

Dr. L Vance, The Other Side of Calvinism, 2002 (Non-Calvinist)

Hugh Y. Reyburn, John Calvin, his life, letters and work, 1910 (Calvinist)

Dr. W. De Greef, The Writings of John Calvin, 1993 (Calvinist)

Dave Hunt video, What Love is This? (Non-Calvinist)

H. Grattan Guinness, Romanism and the Reformation, 1887 (Calvinist)

C. Hutson, Why I disagree with all five points of Calvinism (Non-Calvinist)

R.C. Sproul, Chosen by God, 1986 (Calvinist)

John Macarthur, The Murder of Jesus, 2000 (Calvinist)

Lewis Mumford, The Condition of Man, 1944 (Calvinist)

James F. Billton – True Wisdom Has Two Sides – Calvinism – is it Biblical?, 2001 (Non-Calvinist)

Peter S. Ruckman, Why I am not a Calvinist, 1997 (Non-Calvinist)

Also by James Battell

The Shocking History of the Jesuits (The Society of Jesus)
King James I of England: The King The Vatican Could Not Kill
The Hidden Truth About Freemasonry, The Catholic Church, And The Illuminati
Bible Prophecy Made Simple For Serious Students of Scripture
Did The Catholic Church Order Abraham Lincoln's Assassination?
Is Calvinism and the TULIP Biblical?
The Book of Genesis Commentary (Chapters 1-11)
Watchman Nee, Witness Lee, and Living Stream Ministry: A Critical Analysis of Their Identity as Cult or Church
What Is Speaking In Tongues And Is It Still For Today?
Ephesians KJV Bible Commentary
The Book of Romans Commentary
Philemon Bible Study (Slavery In Scripture)
The Holy Ghost Within The Trinity
The Immaculate Conception ("Deception")
The Book of John KJV Commentary
The Book of Matthew KJV Commentary
The Epistles of John (1-3 John KJV Commentary)
Agent of Grace

Oliver Cromwell: The Last King of England
The Incredible Story of How the Papacy Became Infallible
Under Pius IX and XII
The Book of Luke KJV Commentary
Billy Graham: The Vatican's Right Hand Man